DOUBLE OR TWIN

DOUBLE OR TWIN

A Comedy in Three Acts and Eight Doors

by Roger Leach and Colin Wakefield

DHP
Double Honours Publications

DOUBLE OR TWIN

by Roger Leach and Colin Wakefield.

First published in 2021 by Double Honours Publications.

ISBN 978-1-9160537-4-8

Applications for performance should be made to Colin Wakefield.

colwake@btinternet.com

CAST OF CHARACTERS

me?

DAVE REID (28)	The bridegroom
Mr. REID (28)	DAVE's identical twin
DESMOND (27)	DAVE's best man
FLO (65)	Mother of the REID twins
VALERIE (VAL) (22))	
)	Identical twin sisters
VANESSA (VAN) (22))	
MERRYL (45)	DAVE's mother-in-law
ANGELINA (21)	DAVE's wife
VICAR (70)	An old friend of Flo's

CASTING NOTE: The two sets of identical twins should not be played by real twins. It is necessary for the audience to be able to distinguish clearly between DAVE and REID, and between VAL and VAN, but to believe that others would confuse them.

The **ACTION** of the play takes place one Saturday night and the following morning in FLO's small hotel at Willard's Bottom.

ACT ONE	Saturday 8.30 p.m.
ACT TWO	Saturday 9.15 p.m.
ACT THREE	Sunday 8.00 a.m.

The action is continuous between Acts One and Two. The play can run without the first interval if preferred.

THE SET

The set is on **TWO LEVELS**, but the play may also be staged on one level, with a raised area just a few steps higher representing the upper level. For the one-level version, please see the alternative stage lay-out opposite.

The **GROUND FLOOR** is the entrance hall to a small hotel, with the front door UCR, the reception desk UCL, and a walk-in staff cupboard under the stairs UL. There are two doors, DL and DR, leading to the guests' dining room and to the staff quarters respectively. There is a window to the left of the front door.

The **STAIRCASE** runs along the stage L wall, in one flight to the landing.

Off the **LANDING** there are three equidistant bedroom doors facing the audience. Room 3 is at the top of the stairs (stage L), Room 2 is in the middle, and Room 1 is at the stage R end. Next to Room 1, facing onstage rather than directly to the audience, is the bathroom/W.C. All doors can be locked with keys from either side. The landing overhangs the desk area below, so that characters at the desk cannot see people on the landing, and vice-versa.

UPPER LEVEL

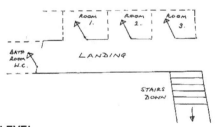

LOWER LEVEL

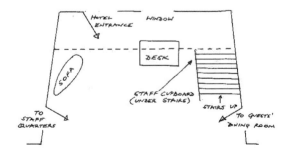

AUDIENCE

THE ONE-LEVEL SET

This version may be preferred by companies with more limited resources, or for touring productions. The stage directions in the script are for the two-level version, but only very minor adjustments need be made for the one-level set (e.g. the exact position of the front door is UR rather than UCR, and the sofa and the window are in different positions). Timings will differ slightly where the characters are going up just a few steps to the landing, rather than up a full flight of stairs.

The entrance hall to a small hotel.

The front door faces the audience UR. There are two doors, DL and DR, leading to the guests' dining room and to the staff quarters respectively. There is a window upstage of the DR door.

Upstage of the DL door is another door to a walk-in staff cupboard, and then three or four steps leading to a raised area (the landing), on which there are three equidistant bedroom doors facing the audience. Room 3 is at the top of the steps (stage L), Room 2 is in the middle, and Room 1 is at the stage R end. Next to Room 1, facing onstage rather than directly to the audience, is the bathroom/W.C. All doors can be locked with keys from either side. The landing has an open balustrade or railing running along the front.

The reception desk stands UCR, with a sofa UCL, between the desk and the steps.

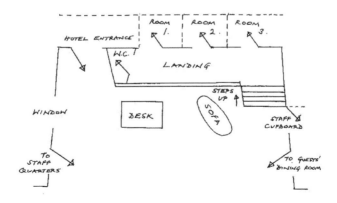

AUDIENCE

Also by Roger Leach and Colin Wakefield

On Your Honour

A Comedy

(5m, 3f. One set)

(Published by Josef Weinberger Plays)

Audience with Murder

A Thriller

(2m, 2f. One set)

(Published by Samuel French)

Double or Twin

ACT ONE

Saturday. 8.30 p.m.

REID is standing with his fishing rod, practising his casting. He is wearing a dark suit, with white shirt and smart tie. He is 28 and runs the hotel with his mother, FLO.

FLO   *(off)* David..? David..?

REID hastily puts his fishing rod aside and goes to the desk.

FLO enters DR. She is 65, dowdy and a spirited moaner.

FLO   David?

REID   Yes, mother?

FLO   What are you doing?

REID   Just writing down a booking for next Friday.

FLO   I hope you've put it in the book.

REID   Yes, mother.

FLO   All reservations go in the book. That's the rule.

REID   That's what I'm doing.

FLO   Oh, it's a life of grief! Have you seen my tablets?

REID   No, mother.

FLO	And my capsules?
REID	No, mother.
FLO	They're not where I left them.
REID	Where was that?
FLO	I don't know, you silly boy. How do I know where I left them if I can't find them? If I knew where I left them they wouldn't be lost, would they? You're not going out fishing tonight, are you?
REID	Yes, it's my night off. You know that.
FLO	But it's that girl's first day. She's only been working here five minutes and already you're off out and about. Dangling a bit of string in the river in the middle of the night. It's the fish I feel sorry for. And we've got guests. The Vicar's back for his annual visit, and Room 2's booked and all. How am I going to cope, me with my angina and my arthritis?
REID	Look –
FLO	You know I can't manage the stairs any more. Not at my time of life.
REID	Mother –
FLO	It was all very well when your father was with us.
REID	Why do you think we got the new girl?

FLO	I know why you got the new girl.
REID	You chose her.
FLO	We had to choose someone. And I didn't notice you making any objections, David Reid. Oh, it's a life of grief!
	FLO *exits DR.* REID *sighs. He opens a box of flies on the desk and starts to check them.*
	VAL *enters from Room 2 with a hoover and a black bin liner. She is 22, attractive and sensible, and is wearing a red blouse with a grey skirt.*
REID	Val. Are you still on the go?
VAL	*(coming downstairs)* I thought I'd give that room a quick going-over, you know.
REID	You're amazing.
VAL	It only took me ten minutes, Mr. Reid. It did need it.
REID	Call me David.
VAL	I've put some flowers in the Vicar's room –
REID	Terrific.
VAL	And fixed that dripping tap in the bathroom.
REID	Where did you find the hoover?
VAL	*(putting the hoover away in the cupboard)* In the cupboard under the stairs. Where it belongs. Is

there anything else before I go and unpack?

REID   How are you at loft conversions?

VAL   Sorry?

REID   Only joking.

VAL   Oh, I see.

REID *laughs. Slight pause.*

VAL   I think I'll go and unpack then, Mr. Reid.

REID   David.

VAL   Er...

REID   You're lovely, Val. Do you know that?

VAL   Mr. Reid –

REID   No, I mean it. You're really something.

VAL   *(firmly)* Mr. Reid. Don't.

REID   Okay, okay. Look, I'm off out fishing in a bit. Sorry to leave you on your own on your first day, but I haven't had a night off for months.

VAL   That's all right.

REID   I've been going mad. It's mother, you see. She can't get up the stairs any more. I am seriously worried about her. I know she moans a lot, but she really does have a dicky ticker. So I try not to upset her. Well, not too much, anyway. Okay,

4

you know the drill. Bookings in the register.
Mother's very hot on that. Her memory's
dreadful. If it's not down in the book, she forgets
she's let the room. Right, who have we got?
(Looking in the register) You've met the Vicar –
he's in Room 3. Keep an eye on him. He's a
regular, stone deaf and easily confused. Then
there's this bloke coming into Room 2, what's
his name? "Smith… Desmond". Said he was best
man at some wedding. He'll be arriving about
nine, so you'll have to deal with him.

VAL   What about keys and things?

REID   Room keys are on the board, that's self-
explanatory. I keep a pass key in case of
emergency. If anyone wants to stay out late, we
keep a couple of house keys on the hook by the
front door, here. So, all you have to do is
remember to lock up last thing before you go to
bed.

VAL   Fine.

REID   Room 1's free if anyone rings, though that's
pretty unlikely now. We have been quite busy,
but over the past few days it seems to have – .

VAL *puts a hand to her left arm in pain.*

VAL   Ow!

REID   What's the matter?

VAL   Vanessa!

REID   What?

VAL	It's my arm. Had this sudden pain.
REID	Are you all right?
VAL	Yes, I'm fine. Don't worry.
REID	Who's this Vanessa when she's at home?
VAL	My twin sister, that's all. Must be her latest boyfriend. Giving her a hard time.
REID	How do you mean?
VAL	Knocking her about a bit.
REID	And you can feel what she feels?
VAL	Only the extremes.
REID	Are you identical then, you and Vanessa?
VAL	Spitting image. We dress differently, of course, and wear our hair differently, but people still muddle us up. It happens all the time. We're not a bit alike in personality, though.
REID	Amazing.
VAL	Not really. A one in two hundred and fifty chance, apparently.
REID	No, I meant… I had a twin too.
VAL	Really?
REID	Yes.

VAL	Identical as well?
REID	Yes.
VAL	Did you say "had"?
REID	Afraid so.
VAL	You mean he's..?
REID	Yes.
VAL	How very sad.
REID	Mm. Mother won't talk about it. It affected her badly. We were only babies, you see, when it happened.
VAL	That's terrible. To lose your twin.
REID	It's a funny thing, though. I sometimes feel he's alive. That he's there. And then I feel… kind of complete, somehow. I can't explain it, really.
VAL	I can understand that.
REID	I get a birthday card from him every year.
VAL	Excuse me?
REID	"To David, love…" – and then the letter D.
VAL	Are you serious?
REID	Not really. It's mother. She sends it. Pretends it's from him. It's her way of keeping his memory alive.

7

VAL	She really has had a tough time, hasn't she? She was telling me this morning as soon as I arrived that she'd had a life of grief.
REID	Yeah, she does milk it a bit.
VAL	No, but what with her arthritis, her depression, and your father dying so young –
REID	She told you that? He's not dead. He ran off with a cocktail waitress from Weston-super-Mare.
VAL	I feel sorry for her. She must be a very sad lady.
FLO	*(shouting, off)* Valerie!
REID	"Oh, it's a life of grief!"
	VAL *laughs.* FLO *enters DR.*
FLO	Valerie. What is your spare uniform doing in your room?
VAL	Well –
FLO	Go and fetch it at once. Staff uniforms belong in the Staff Changing Cupboard, where they belong. *(Pointing to the cupboard)* There.
VAL	Sorry, Mrs. Reid.
	VAL *exits DR.*
FLO	Oh, it's a – You watch that one, David Reid. She's a little husky, she is.
REID	I think she's sweet.

FLO
Sweet? Too sweet. You wait. She'll soon show herself in her true contours. I know her sort. Mincing about in tiny skirts. Misplacing her body to men. She's nothing but a hypochondriac.

REID
Mother...

FLO
Are you going fishing or aren't you?

REID
I'm just off.

FLO
Go, then. Leave me to manage. A poor, lonely old woman.

REID
Come on, mother. I'll be back early morning. As usual.

FLO
I can't bear to think of my boy risking life and limb out at night in foul weather. What would I do if I lost you?

VAL enters DR. She carries the spare uniform (another red blouse and grey skirt) on a hanger.

REID
Mother, I'm twenty-eight, it's a warm evening, and I promise to keep away from the sharks. All right?

He turns to go DR.

VAL
'Bye, Mr. Reid. Have a good fish.

REID
I haven't gone yet. Just going to get my bait.

He exits DR.

FLO	His smelly old fishing clothes remain in the Staff Changing Cupboard. Where they belong.
	VAL *is about to open the cupboard door when* FLO *interrupts.*
FLO	Have you done the Vicar's supper yet?
VAL	Nearly ready, Mrs. Reid.
FLO	Well, hurry up. He'll be ravished by now.
VAL	Yes, Mrs. Reid.
	She hooks the uniform over the cupboard door instead of putting it away and exits DL.
	The VICAR *enters from Room 3. He is 70.*
VICAR	My dear Flo, there you are. How are you?
FLO	Not at all well, Vicar. But thanks for asking.
VICAR	Marvellous.
FLO	My legs are giving me a lot of gyp.
VICAR	Good, good. That's what I like to hear.
FLO	*(louder)* And the doctor says if I don't cut down on my celestial intake I'm heading for a cadillac arrest.
VICAR	Oh, dear. And how are the legs?
FLO	Giving me gyp, Vicar. Anyway, it's nice to see you back.

VICAR	Snack? I'd love one. Thank you very much.
FLO	Watch my lips, Vicar. *(Close to him)* It's nice to see you back.
VICAR	Ah! Always a pleasure, my dear. Every year, you know me. I like to be with you on the anniversary of your sad loss.
FLO	Twenty-eight years ago, Vicar. Don't remind me. The christening of my little twins. How can I ever forgive myself? I popped into the vestry, if you remember, to check that my hat was on straight. And when I got back, there he was – gone. Spirited away. Egg-coddler and all. My little David. Never to be seen again. I'd saved up, you see, to buy two silver egg-coddlers for their christening, each engraved with his own little name. It was all my fault –
VICAR	No, no, no.
FLO	And the David I have now bears the name of his lost twin brother, the real David, to keep his memory alive in my heart. So now I have two Davids, one in my heart and one in my... hotel. And do you know, Vicar, I send a birthday card to this David every year from his little twin, the lost David, God rest his soul.
VICAR	No, Flo, no. Take comfort from my vision. The dream I had the night the boy was lost. Your David is alive. Share my faith. Why do you think I return here year after year? To comfort you, yes. But also because I know that the time will come when the prophesy in my vision will be fulfilled:

> "Girls, not boys, lead the way –
> "Double joys: redemption day!"

Always puzzled me that, the girls bit. But I shall know it when I see it.

FLO   I wish I had your faith, Vicar. You're a good man in a wicked world, but it's nice to see you anyway. Now, the new girl's got your supper ready. Off you go.

VICAR   *(going)* "Girls, not boys". Mm. God moves in mysterious ways.

He exits DL.

FLO   Vision? Cobblers!

She exits DR.

VANESSA *enters at the front door. She is VAL's identical twin. She is wearing a smart coat over a red dress and carries a small overnight bag. She wears her hair long. She rings the reception bell and rubs her left arm.*

VAL *enters DL.*

VAL   Vanessa!

VAN   *(expansive)* Val, hi!

VAL   What are you doing here? Are you all right?

VAL *rubs her left arm too.*

VAN   It's Gary, the bastard.

VAL	Started getting violent, did he?
VAN	No. Why?
VAL	Well, your arm. I thought maybe…
VAN	My arm? Oh, you felt that too, did you? Sorry. No, that wasn't Gary. I banged it on the car door.
VAL	So, what went wrong?
VAN	Gary's gone mad. I can't go back to the flat. He's taken up transcendental meditation, turned teetotal, and given up sex.
VAL	Pity. Wasn't bad in bed.
VAN	How do you know?
VAL	I knew you'd hurt your arm, didn't I?
VAN	You mean..? *(VAL gives her a look)* Cheeky monkey!
VAL	*(laughing)* Not serious.
VAN	So, any dishy men about?
VAL	Vanessa, you are impossible. What happened to that last bloke you were going out with?
VAN	Who, Rob?
VAL	No –
VAN	Bill?
VAL	No –

VAN   Sam?

VAL   That's the one.

VAN   Oh, he was ages ago.

VAL   I can't keep up with you, I really can't.

VAN   They were all so boring.

VAL   You're never satisfied, that's your trouble.

VAN   Valerie, they all had the wrong name.

VAL   Oh, not that Desmond nonsense again.

VAN   Look, you may laugh, but you know the only men who really turn me on are called Desmond. Remember that lovely Desmond Longstaff we met on holiday in Skegness? He was divine.

VAL   He didn't last long, though, did he?

VAN   He was a G.I.

VAL   He was Scottish.

VAN   Yeah, G.I. "Geographically Impossible". We were only fifteen and his father took him home to Motherwell. Val, I'm desperate for a Desmond.

VAL   Go and find one, then.

VAN   There aren't many about nowadays. Desmond Tutu's married. Anyway, I'm not too good with clergymen. They tend to want to get up early on

Sundays. Des Lynam's given up *Countdown*.
And Desmond Morris – you know, the Naked
Ape – he's got some very funny ideas about
primate behaviour. I did meet a lovely one on the
bus the other day. We got on fine for a couple of
hours, but it turned out he'd had a sex change
and his real name was Desdemona.

*[Alternative 'Desmonds' may be substituted as
desired or necessary]*

FLO   *(off)* Valerie!

VAN   Who's that?

VAL   The boss. Won't be a tick.

              VAL *exits DR.*

              VICAR *enters DL, his napkin tucked into his
collar.*

VICAR   Ah.

VAN   Hello.

VICAR   Where's the salt and pepper, my dear?

VAN   I don't know.

VICAR   Flo? Don't know.

VAN   Shall I call Val?

VICAR   And a very charming name it is too. I'm looking
for the salt and pepper, Val.

VAN	I'm her sister, sorry.
VICAR	Kitchen trolley? Thank you, m'dear.

He exits DL.

VAN takes off her coat and puts it down, revealing a dress the same colour and design as VAL's blouse, but with a shorter skirt.

VAL enters DR.

VAL	Sorry about that. When the dragon calls, you jump.
VAN	Where am I sleeping, then?
VAL	What?
VAN	Can I kip in your room?
VAL	No, you can't.
VAN	Why not?
VAL	I'm not allowed. House rules.
VAN	I need your help, Val. It's only for one night.
VAL	No, Van. Definitely not. I'm in the family quarters, right next to Mrs. Reid's room. She's made it quite clear to me: no visitors.
VAN	But I'm your sister. Anyway, it's a hotel, isn't it? Aren't there any empty rooms?
VAL	That's not the point. I can't just... You don't

	know what she's like. She'd go mad. It's more than my job's worth, Van. I'm sorry, but I can't. I just can't.
VAN	But I've got nowhere to sleep! Who else can I turn to? *(Breaking down in tears)* Where can I go?
VAL	Shh, quiet! Calm down.
	VAN *calms down slightly.*
VAL	You have to understand, I can't just –
	VAN *starts to wail.*
VAL	All right, all right, you can stay.
VAN	*(recovering immediately)* Val, you're a treas.
VAL	But on the strict understanding that it's only for tonight. And for God's sake don't let anyone see you. There'd be hell to pay. Right, I know there's one room free.
	She goes to the desk.
VAN	I'll give you some money.
VAL	Don't be daft. *(Looking in the register)* The Vicar's in Room 3 –
VAN	Oh, I met him. Little poppet. He was looking for the salt.
VAL	Eh?

VAN	Don't worry. He thought I was you.
	She follows VAL *behind the desk.*
VAL	And there's a chap coming into Room 2, called Smith, Des... des... nobody in Room 1. *(She slams the register shut)* You can stay there. Room 1. But if the old dragon sees you, I lose my job. All right?
VAN	I'll be as good as gold, I promise. You won't know I'm here. You're a star, Val, you really are.
	She gives VAL *a kiss.*
FLO	*(off)* Valerie!
VAL	Get down, quick!
VAN	What?
VAL	It's her.
	FLO *enters DR.*
	VAN *has to duck down instead of* VAN.
VAN	Who? *(Seeing FLO)* Hoo-hoo!
FLO	Valerie.
VAN	Yes, Mrs...
VAL	*(whispers)* "Reid".
VAN	Reid.

FLO	Have you seen my – ? I thought I told you that uniform belongs in the Staff Changing Cupboard, where it belongs.
VAN	Blimey O'Reilly!
FLO	Don't you speak to me like that, you little trolley! And put your hair back up. This is a respectable house, this is.
VAN	Yes, Mrs. –
FLO	Oh, it's a life of grief!

FLO *exits DR.*

VAL *reappears from behind the desk.*

VAL	See what I mean? Come on. Upstairs. Quick.

They go upstairs.

VAN	And you said you liked this job.
VAL	I never said I liked it. It's the only one I could get.
VAN	Rather you than me.
VAL	Right. Room 1.
VAN	Thanks, Val.
VAL	The bathroom's just there.
VAN	That's handy.

Double or Twin

They exit into Room 1.

REID enters DR with bait and collects his rod to pack it up.

VICAR enters DL.

REID   Good supper, Vicar?

VICAR   No, I've just had it, thank you.

REID   Dear oh dear.

VICAR   Every year, yes.

REID   God in Heaven.

VICAR   Not in Devon, no. Here. Every year. Where are you off to, David?

REID   Dry stone walling, Vicar.

VICAR   Good fishing there, is it?

REID   Something like that.

VICAR   Under my hat, oh yes. Won't tell a soul. Well, good luck. I'm off to bed. Big day tomorrow.

REID   Good night, Vicar.

VICAR   *(to* REID*)* "Girls, not boys, lead the way…" *(Going upstairs)* Always puzzled me that, the girls bit. But I'll know it when I see it.

He exits into Room 3.

REID	Good grief.
	VAN *enters from Room 1.*
VAL	*(from Room 1: stage whisper)* Vanessa! Come back!
VAN	Forgotten my coat.
	She closes the door.
REID	Is this it?
	VAN *reaches half-way down the stairs. She and* REID *see each other and stop in their tracks.*
VAN	Hello!
REID	Well, look at you!
VAN	Mmm...
REID	You look ravishing.
VAN	You're not so bad yourself.
REID	What have you done to your hair?
VAN	Do you like it?
REID	I do, yes. And that's a terrific dress.
VAN	Thank you. Going out?
REID	Yes. Fishing.

VAN	See you later, maybe.
REID	*(pleasantly surprised)* Maybe.
VAN	I'll look forward to that.
REID	Sorry I'm off out.
VAN	Well, hurry back!
REID	Right. Yes. Er… well, I suppose I'd better go and change. Fishing. You know.

He exits into the cupboard.

VAN *collects her coat.*

VAL *enters from Room 1.*

VAL	Vanessa!
FLO	*(off)* Valerie!

VAL *hastily returns to Room 1 and shuts the door.*

FLO *enters DR.*

FLO	*(crossing DL)* Where's my cod liver oil tablets? Have you seen my cod liver oil tablets?

She exits DL.

VAN *holds out* FLO*'s bottle of tablets from the desk.*

Double or Twin

VAL *enters from Room 1 and leans over the banister.*

VAL   Vanessa!

VAN   What?

VAL   Come up!

VAN   Stop fussing.

VAL   I told you to keep out of the way.

VAN   It doesn't matter. They all think I'm you. Bit of a laugh, really. Just like school.

VAL   And who ended up getting expelled? You tell me that.

VAN   Val, come on. It did wonders for your street cred.

VAL   While you stayed behind and failed my O-levels.

VAN   Is there any food? I'm starving.

VAL   What do you think this is, a hotel?

VAN   Where's the kitchen?

VAL   No, you come up here. I'll get you something.

VAN   *(going upstairs)* You're a marvel, do you know that? What shall I do with these tablets?

VAL   I'd better have them.

She takes the tablets from VAN.

REID enters from the cupboard, dressed for fishing.

REID   *(calling out)* Goodbye, mother!

VAN   'Byee!

                VAL steps behind VAN *to avoid being seen.* REID *turns upstage.*

REID   Oh. 'Bye, Val. Love the dress.

                He exits by the front door.

FLO   *(off)* Valerie!

                VAN *covers up the lower part of her dress with her coat by folding it over the banister.*

                FLO *enters DL.*

FLO   Valerie! Where's my tablets?

VAL   *(putting her hand, with the tablets, through* VAN*'s arm)* Here, Mrs. Reid.

VAN   Here, Mrs. Reid.

VAL   *(sotto voce)* Two, three...

VAL/VAN   *(loudly, together)* Here, Mrs. Reid.

FLO   All right, all right. I'm not deaf.

	VAL *throws the tablets over the banister.* FLO *catches them.*
FLO	Yes, go on. Throw them at me. Thank you very much. I thought I told you to put your hair up.
VAL	*(sotto voce)* Two, three…
VAL/VAN	*(together)* Yes, Mrs. Reid.
	Both pairs of hands put up VAN*'s hair.*
FLO	*(confused)* Oh, me heart!
	She exits DR.
VAL	Go on, inside! I'll fetch you something to eat.
	She comes downstairs.
VAN	Val…
VAL	What?
VAN	*(warmly)* Thanks.
	She exits into Room 1.
VAL	*(smiling)* "Oh, it's a life of grief!"
	She exits DL.
	The front door opens sharply. Enter MERRYL. *She is 45, draconian but not unattractive, and smartly dressed. She is* DAVE*'s mother-in-law.*

She is followed by DESMOND. *He is 27,*
DAVE*'s best man, quite shy, and with a strong*
moral code. He is meekly carrying his and
DAVE*'s suitcases.*

MERRYL   Yes, I know he's your best friend, Desmond, and
          I know you grew up together in that
          'establishment'. So you're bound to defend him.
          You are his best man, after all. But I had a
          feeling from the very beginning that this
          wedding would be a fiasco. *(Ringing the bell*
          imperiously: "Ping!") My Angelina. My only
          daughter. And sole heir to the family firm. As if
          it wasn't bad enough her marrying a creature like
          David. But then to eat shellfish at the reception,
          with her allergic history. I've always told her:
          "Never trust a prawn, an oyster or a winkle!"
          And now she's hospitalised on her wedding
          night, the poor darling. Mind you, that could be
          seen as a blessing, with that dreadful young man
          I am now obliged to call a son-in-law. So, the
          first night's off! He will stay with you here
          whilst I take his place at Angelina's bedside.

          FLO *enters DR.*

MERRYL   Ah. You must be the proprietor. My name is
          Philpott. We need an extra room.

FLO   I shall have to check the book.

          She consults the register.

MERRYL   We already have one reservation – *(Looking over*
          FLO*'s shoulder)* – in the name of Smith.

Double or Twin

FLO	*(suspicious)* Smith?
MERRYL	There it is – Room 2. I see Room 1's free. We'll take that. Of course, I shall need to inspect the accommodation. Desmond, you stay here.
	She heads upstairs.
FLO	"Smith" did you say the name was?
DES	That's right.
FLO	Are you sure?
DES	Of course I'm sure.
FLO	She just said her name was Philpott. This is a respectable house, this is.
	MERRYL *bellows over the banister.*
MERRYL	Oh, for Heaven's sake, I'm not staying here.
FLO	Suit yourself.
MERRYL	It's for my son-in-law.
FLO	*(to DES)* I suppose his name's Smith too, is it?
DES	No, Reid.
FLO	Reid?
DES	Yes.
FLO	That's my name.

DES	Is it now?
FLO	Yes. Has been for years. Have you got a pen?
DES	No, sorry.

MERRYL *exits into Room 2.*

VAN *enters from Room 1 and exits into the bathroom.*

FLO	Oh, me poor old legs.

She exits DR.

MERRYL *enters from Room 2.*

MERRYL	That's fine, Desmond. Bring up the cases.
DES	Yes, Mrs. Philpott.

He starts upstairs with the cases. MERRYL *takes a quick look round the door of Room 1.*

MERRYL	Not where I'd have chosen to stay, but still.

During the following, DES *takes the cases into Room 2, then follows* MERRYL *back downstairs.*

MERRYL	Now, Desmond. You know my opinion of David. He's a bounder. Loud, unreliable and sex-mad. Angelina seems to be able to keep him under control, but I don't trust him on his own for a moment, particularly on his wedding night. So tonight I am depending on you. Any hanky-

panky and I shall hold you to account. And you
know what that means, don't you, Desmond, as
an employee of Philpott's Potted Pastes? I trust I
make myself clear?

DES   Yes, Mrs. Philpott.

MERRYL   I'm not a hard woman, Desmond, God knows
                I'm not. You see this money?

DES   Yes, Mrs. Philpott.

MERRYL   It is five hundred pounds.

DES   Yes, Mrs. Philpott.

MERRYL   In cash. Now. This is my little contribution
                towards the honeymoon. I was intending to give
                it to Angelina – you know what David's like
                with money – but now I am entrusting it to you.

DES   To me, Mrs. Philpott?

MERRYL   Yes. I know you are an orphan, with a
                disadvantaged childhood, and that you grew up
                in a home, but I am trusting you nevertheless.

DES   Thank you very much, Mrs. Philpott.

                *There is the sound of an unusual car horn
                outside.*

MERRYL   Oh, my God.

DES   *(going to the window)* It's Dave.

MERRYL   I told him to wait at the hospital until I got back.
              Wretched boy. Desmond.

DES   Yes, Mrs. Philpott?

MERRYL   Remember what I said. I want David kept under
              strict control. You know what I mean – girls and
              so forth. I shall hold you personally responsible,
              Desmond. Do I make myself clear?

DES   Yes, Mrs. Philpott.

MERRYL   My daughter is not going to be made a fool of.

DES   No, Mrs. Philpott.

MERRYL   Standards must be maintained.

              She exits by the front door.

DES   Three bags full, Mrs. Philpott.

              He visibly relaxes.

              VICAR *enters from Room 3, dressed in his
              nightshirt, still with dog collar, and crosses to
              the bathroom.*

VICAR   *(to* DES, *below)* Good evening.

DES   Hello.

VICAR   Nightshirt. Sorry.

DES   Don't mind me.

VICAR	Need a tinkle. Lots of noise out here. Couldn't sleep.
DES	Not surprised.
VICAR	*(before he reaches the bathroom door)* Occupied? Is it? Thank you very much. Goodnight.

He returns to Room 3.

DAVE REID enters at the front door. He is REID's identical twin. He is dressed in a suit exactly like REID's.

DES	Dave! Good to see you, mate.

They perform their "Barnado Boys" ritual: a brief handshake and slap sequence.

DES	How's Ange?
DAVE	Angel by name, mate, angel by nature.
DES	I told you she was the one.
DAVE	I'm in heaven, Des. What she's done for me, that woman.
DES	Changed your life.
DAVE	I know I've had a lot of birds, and got a bit of a reputation for myself, but I never felt anything for any of them, do you know what I mean? I didn't love them. I thought I did, but now I've met Ange I realise I didn't. She's magic, Des. I

know it sounds a bit soft, but she's... she's the
one I want to grow old with.

DES   Over the worst then, is she?

DAVE   What?

DES   She's in with a chance of making it to old age?

DAVE   Eh?

DES   How is she, for God's sake?

DAVE   Fine. Out tomorrow morning, they reckon.

DES   Terrific.

DAVE   Old Fish-Paste was in a bit of a hurry.

DES   Excuse me, that's my boss you're talking about.
And you did promise to stay by Angelina's
bedside, you know.

DAVE   Yeah, well, she was asleep, wasn't she. They'd
knocked her out. Didn't see much point in sitting
next to a bed with a beautiful bird in it. Thought
a few bevvies with my best man were in order.

DES   What are you like?

DAVE   See any decent pubs on your way here?

DES   I was being ear-bashed at the time by Merryl the
Peril. Your sweet-tempered mother-in-law.
Which reminds me. She gave me this, for you
and Ange.

DAVE   What is it?

DES   Five hundred quid. For the honeymoon.

DAVE   Blimey.

DES   Yeah. Generous, eh?

DAVE   Five hundred quid.

DES   You'd better have it. Merryl half-reckons I'll nick it.

DAVE   Oh, I get it. "Barnado Boy Strikes Again!" I've had all that as well. Look Des, you hang on to it. You know what I'm like. Can't keep anything for five minutes.

DES   You've kept that blasted egg-coddler with you all these years. Ever since I've known you.

DAVE   *(producing it from his pocket)* Ah, well, my egg-coddler. That's different. My only connection with my Mum, that is. *(Reading)* "David Reid, 22nd of April 19[93], from your ever-loving Mum". I may have lost her as a nipper, Des old son, but I know she's out there somewhere.

FLO *enters DR, with a pen.*

FLO   I've got the pen.

DES   Ah.

FLO   *(to* DAVE*)* Haven't you gone yet?

DAVE   Gone? I've only just arrived.

FLO   *(giving him the pen)* You'd better take care of
              this. Room 1. Reid. Write it down. This gent's in
              Room 2. And don't forget to tell him, if he's out
              late the front door key belongs on the hook there,
              where it belongs.

              She exits DR.

DAVE   Write it down? Write what down?

DES   Forget it. She's one slice short of a loaf. Let's go
              and unpack.

              He collects keys 1 and 2 from the board as
              DAVE *leads the way upstairs.*

DES   She's probably overworked. Looks like she's
              running this place without any help.

DAVE   What, no tasty little chambermaids?

DES   Hey!

DAVE   What?

DES   You're a married man now, remember.

DAVE   Only just.

              VAN *enters from the bathroom.*

VAN   Hello again. Who's your little friend?

DAVE   Blimey!

34

VAN	I'm just getting something to eat. I'm starving.
DAVE	Well, a girl's got to eat.
VAN	Do you fancy a little something?
DAVE	Is that an offer?
DES	*(to* DAVE*)* Hey!
VAN	Could be.
DAVE	Well…
VAN	You're not going out, then?
DAVE	We were thinking of having a few jars later on, if you fancied joining –
DES	But I'm afraid we have a bit of business to discuss.
VAN	Oh. Well, give me a shout if you want me.
	She goes downstairs and exits DL.
DAVE	Things are looking up.
DES	I don't believe this.
DAVE	Don't worry, Des old cocker. Only window shopping.
DES	Oh, yeah?
DAVE	Yeah.

DES	It's not worth it, Dave. For either of us. Please.
DAVE	*(lightly)* Okay, okay.

DES *exits into Room 2.*

VICAR, *now in his dressing-gown and slippers, enters from Room 3 to go to the bathroom, as* DAVE *is about to follow* DES *into Room 2.*

VICAR	No fish, then?
DAVE	What?
VICAR	No fish.
DAVE	Bad luck, mate.
VICAR	Sorry to hear that.

DAVE *exits into Room 2.*

VAN *enters DL with a plate of scrambled eggs.*

VICAR	No fish.
VAN	No, eggs.
VICAR	Legs? I know, she's having a lot of trouble.

VAN *comes upstairs.*

VAN	Could you unzip my dress, Vicar?
VICAR	Dear child!

VAN	I can't reach the back.
VICAR	I'm a man of the cloth.
VAN	Don't worry, it's all above board. I used to live next to a theological college.
VICAR	Oh well, if you say so. *(He unzips* VAN*'s dress at the back)* Bless my soul.
VAN	Thank you very much.
	VICAR *exits into Room 3.*
	VAN *shimmies off her dress, down to her petticoat. She exits into Room 1.*
	VAL *enters DL, crossing to DR.*
	VICAR *re-enters immediately from Room 3 to go to the bathroom.*
VICAR	That was a quick change.
VAL	Hello, Vicar. Just off to bed?
VICAR	Which theological college was that?
VAL	I beg your pardon?
VICAR	Which theological college?
VAL	Absolutely.
	She exits DR.

VICAR   Poor girl, must be deaf.

                 He exits into the bathroom.

                 DAVE *enters from Room 2, followed by* DES.

DAVE   A bit sparse. I'm going to have a look at mine.

                 He tries the door of Room 1 with his key. Finding it's not locked, he opens the door and looks in.

                 He leaves the key in the lock.

DES   How is it?

DAVE   Bloody hell!

DES   What's wrong?

DAVE   Nothing.

DES   Let's have a look.

                 DAVE *shuts the door.*

DAVE   No, it's fine. Fine.

DES   You all right?

DAVE   *(forced yawn)* Just tired, mate, that's all. Been one hell of a day. Need to get my head down for a bit. Tell you what. Meet you for a drink in half an hour, eh?

DES   *(slightly puzzled)* Yeah. Okay. See you downstairs.

Double or Twin

DES *and* DAVE *open their doors simultaneously.* VAN *giggles.*

VAN   *(off)* Ooh, hello!

DAVE   Shh!

DES *exits into Room 2.*

DAVE   Can I come in?

VAN   *(off)* If you like.

DAVE *exits into Room 1.*

DES *re-enters immediately from Room 2. He goes to the door of Room 1 and knocks.*

DES   Dave. *(No reply)* Dave!

DAVE   *(off)* What?

DES   Window shopping, eh? Look, I've got a responsibility here, you know what I mean? *(Pause)* Right, if you're not back in my room in ten seconds, I'm contacting you-know-who at the hospital.

He exits into Room 2.

VAL *enters DR, in time to see DAVE coming out of Room 1, leaving the door ajar. DAVE does not see her.*

VAN   *(off)* Don't be long.

Double or Twin

DAVE *exits into Room 2.*

VAL — Well, really! *(Storming upstairs)* Vanessa, this isn't fair. It isn't fair and it isn't funny. And I'm putting a stop to it now.

She slams shut the door of Room 1 and locks VAN in, leaving the key in the lock.

VAN — *(off)* Val..! Val..!

DAVE *enters from Room 2.*

DAVE — Boring little do-gooder! *(Seeing VAL before he can close the door)* That was a quick change.

VAL — That was a quick fish.

DAVE — Fish?

VAL — This has got to stop, Mr. Reid.

DAVE — Are we going back in, then?

VAL — Certainly not.

DAVE — You've changed your tune.

VAL — *(knowing what he means)* Have I?

DAVE *approaches VAL for a kiss.*

VAL — Mr. Reid!

She slaps him.

Double or Twin

DES *enters from Room 2.*

VAL   Stop it!

DAVE   What have I done?

VAL   You know perfectly well what you've done.

DAVE   I'm sorry, I –

DES   Come on, Dave. You come with me. *(Marching him downstairs)* I think a pint is in order.

DAVE   But –

DES   We'll find a nice country pub. Wooden beams, horse brasses, Aussie lager –

DAVE   All right, all right, I'm coming. It was only a bit of fun. No harm done.

DES   I'm sorry about my friend, Miss… um… Sorry.

DAVE   Sorry.

DES *takes a key and they exit by the front door.*

VAL   *(puzzled)* "Friend"?

She goes to the door of Room 1, unlocks it and calls to VAN.

VAL   Vanessa!

VAN *enters from Room 1.*

VAN	What?
VAL	Out!
VAN	Eh?
VAL	You heard. You've only been here five minutes and already you're trying to get my boss into bed. I told you, I'll lose my job.
VAN	Your boss?
VAL	You promised to behave, Vanessa. I'm livid, I really am.
VAN	Did you say boss?
VAL	Yes. Mr. Reid.
VAN	Ooh, I thought he was a guest. He's ever so dishy. Sorry.
VAL	Yes, and I'm sorry too. It's my first day here and already he thinks I'm a nymphomaniac. I'm going to have to work overtime now to re-establish anything like a professional relationship with him. You don't realise the damage you do, Vanessa, you and your silly games. I'm sorry, but you really will have to leave.
VAN	All right, all right, I'll go. Just calm down. I'll get dressed.
VAL	*(a little surprised)* Are you sure?
VAN	Sure I'm sure.

VAL	Where will you go?
VAN	Back to Gary, I suppose. I've got the car. I'll be home by midnight.
	She exits into Room 1.
VAL	Vanessa…
VAN	*(off)* Don't worry. I'll be all right.
	VICAR *enters from the bathroom.*
FLO	*(off)* Valerie!
VAL	*(to* VICAR*'s face)* Oh, God.
VICAR	No, my dear, but close.
	VAL *hurries downstairs.*
VICAR	Strange girl.
	He exits into Room 3.
	FLO *enters DR.*
FLO	Valerie.
VAL	Yes, Mrs. Reid?
FLO	Have you locked up yet?
VAL	I was just about to, Mrs. Reid.

FLO   I assume you'll be wanting an early call
           tomorrow.

VAL   Um –

FLO   You're not a churchgoer, then? I had to give up
           religion when my legs got bad. But if more
           people went to church we'd have less of this
           immortality. You've put your hair up again, I
           see. That's something. And I thought I told you
           that uniform belongs in the Staff Changing
           Cupboard, where it belongs. Oh, it's a life of
           grief!

           She exits DR.

VAL   Vanessa, hurry up. The coast's clear.

           VAN *enters from Room 1 and comes downstairs.*

VAN   I'm ever so sorry about all this. I just can't help
           myself sometimes.

VAL   Sometimes!

VAN   I really hope you don't lose your job, Val. I'd
           hate that. Well, I'd... er... get to bed now if I
           were you.

VAL   Don't worry, I'm off this minute. I can hardly
           keep my eyes open. Give us a ring tomorrow.

VAN   Right, then, I'm away. 'Bye.

           They kiss cheeks.

VAL	'Bye.

VAN exits by the front door.

VICAR enters from Room 3 with the Church Times and heads downstairs.

VICAR	Isn't it time you were in bed, m'dear?
VAL	Got to lock up first, Vicar.

She gets a key from the hook and locks the front door. She puts the key back and puts the spare uniform in the cupboard.

VICAR	Me too. Couldn't sleep. Big day tomorrow. Got a feeling in my water.
VAL	Yes, Vicar. I'm just going to turn down your bed.

She goes upstairs.

VICAR	I owe it to Flo, you know, I owe it to Flo. God knows I do.

> "Girls, not boys, lead the way –
> "Double joys: redemption day!"

VAL exits into Room 3.

VICAR settles down on the sofa to read his Church Times. Tapping is heard at the window as VAN tries to attract his attention. VICAR is confused. Finally he sees VAN.

VICAR	Oh, I thought… Didn't you..? Ah well, never mind.

He collects a key and lets her in at the front door.

VAN   Sorry, Vicar. Locked myself out.

She re-locks the door, but leaves the key in the lock.

VICAR   It's the girls bit I don't understand.

VAN   Did you see a uniform hanging up here, Vicar?

VICAR   And why should they be first?

VAN   Vicar. The uniform.

VICAR   Um... *(Indicating cupboard)* Didn't you just put it away in the... er..?

VAN   Of course I did. Silly me!

VICAR   And how will I know?

VAN   I shouldn't worry about it, Vicar.

She goes into the cupboard to change.

VAL *enters from Room 3.*

VICAR   But I do worry, my dear.

VAL   *(coming downstairs)* Worry about what, Vicar?

VICAR   *(startled)* Ah!

VAL   Are you all right?

VICAR	Didn't you..? I mean, how did you..? In the cupboard... The uniform... Dear Lord!
VAL	I should try and get some sleep if I were you, Vicar.

She exits DR.

VAN enters from the cupboard, dressed in the spare uniform and putting her hair up.

VICAR	*(seeing* VAN*)* Dear God! It's a vision!
VAN	I should try and get some sleep if I were you, Vicar.

VICAR stumbles in amazed excitement up the stairs to Room 3.

VICAR	"Girls, not boys lead the way..." These must be the girls! But lead the way where?

He exits into Room 3.

There is a tap at the front door.

VAN	Who is it?
DAVE	It's Dave.
VAN	Who, Mr. Reid?
DAVE	Yes. Let me in.

VAN unlocks the front door.

Enter DAVE.

VAN	Hello.
DAVE	Hello.
VAN	What have you done with your friend?
DAVE	I gave him the slip at the pub.
VAN	So it's just us now.
DAVE	Um... yes.
VAN	I think everyone else has gone to bed.

She lets down her hair.

DAVE	Oh, yes?
VAN	Room 1, then?
DAVE	Ah...

The phone rings. Neither of them answers it.

VAN	Are you going to get that or shall I?
DAVE	I'm not going to.
VAN	You go and get ready, then. I'll be up in a minute.
DAVE	Look...
VAN	Go on!

DAVE *starts up the stairs.*

Double or Twin

FLO, *in her nightgown and curlers, enters DR,
unnoticed.*

VAN *answers the phone.*

VAN   Hello. Reception. Valerie speaking ... No, we're
                    fully booked ... *(She starts unbuttoning her
                    blouse)* ... The last double's just been taken ...
                    No twins either, sorry. 'Byee!

                    DAVE *stops in his tracks at the top of the stairs
                    as he sees* FLO.

                    VAN *takes out a negligée from her bag and
                    models it against herself.*

VAN   I'm taking you to paradise, Mr. Reid.

                    She starts up the stairs.

FLO   Over my dead body you are!

                    VAN *and* DAVE *freeze.*

                    CURTAIN

                    *[This interval is optional. The action is
                    continuous]*

ACT TWO

FLO   Come down here this instant, David Reid.

DAVE *comes downstairs.*

FLO   I thought you said you were going out.

DAVE   What's that got to do with you?

FLO   It's got everything to do with me, young man. Sneaking back under cover of darkness to arrange your amorous parlez-vouze. Not in this house, you don't. I warned you she was a husky. Well, I was right. I forbid you to go anywhere near her again.

DAVE   And I suggest you mind your own business.

FLO   How dare you speak to me like that!

DAVE   I shall speak to you exactly how I like.

FLO   Ooh, you've been corrupted, David. Drawn into the vile web of pre-maritime sex. Sucked into the murky waters of wickedness and vice. Sully not the purity of your marriage bed, my son.

DAVE   Blimey!

FLO   And you, you little Charlotte! I knew as soon as I clamped eyes on you that you were fast and loose. With your mincing ways and your mini-skirts, and your hair up one minute and down the next like there was no tomorrow. I want you out of here first thing in the morning. I'll pack your bags myself. And you, my son, are spending the night with me.

DAVE *is speechless at this prospect.*

VAN	Look, Mrs. ... um...
FLO	You're sacked.
VAN	I'm ever so sorry.
FLO	Dismissed.
DAVE	It was my fault. Really.
FLO	You hold your tongue.
VAN	It won't happen again.
FLO	Too right it won't. You'll be elsewhere, where you belong. We'll have to find you a room. You're not sleeping anywhere near him tonight. Bring me the book.
VAN	The book?
FLO	The book.
VAN	The book...
FLO	David. The book!
DAVE	The book?
FLO	What's the matter with you people?

She goes to the desk.

DAVE	She's mad. Nutty as a fruitcake.
VAN	Well, so long as it doesn't run in the family.
DAVE	Eh?
FLO	Room 1's free.
DAVE	Is it?
VAN	Shh!
FLO	*(to* VAN*)* I'll put you in there for the night. *(To* DAVE*)* And I want you washed and undressed immediately.
DAVE	You what?
FLO	You're coming to bed with me.
DAVE	Bed..?
FLO	Your father would turn in his grave.
DAVE	*(to* VAN*)* She's round the bend.
VAN	*(sotto voce)* Just humour her. Do as she says.
DAVE	Eh?
	FLO *makes to go DR, expecting* DAVE *to follow her.*
FLO	Come on.
VAN	*(still to* DAVE*)* I'll be upstairs. If you get

undressed down here, you'll be ready for me,
won't you.

FLO *pulls* DAVE *by the ear.*

FLO   You'll thank me for this in the morning, David
           Reid. *(To* VAN*)* And you, you little trumpet –
           Room 1.

VAN   *(ambiguously, to both* FLO *and* DAVE*)* Room 1.

DAVE   *(confirming to* VAN*)* Room 1.

           FLO *drags* DAVE *off DR.*

DAVE   Ow!

           VAN, *still anticipating a night of bliss, turns and
           runs up the stairs.*

           DES *enters at the front door.*

DES   *(cross)* Where's Dave?

VAN   Oh, it's you.

DES   Is he with you?

VAN   Not yet.

DES   This isn't a joke, you know. Is he upstairs?

VAN   He's gone to his room.

DES   So where are you off to?

VAN   Room 1.

DES	You do realise, don't you, that he's a married man?
VAN	Who, Mr. Reid?
DES	Yes.
VAN	Married?
DES	Yes.
VAN	She never said.
DES	What?
VAN	Well, I'd never have... you know... if I'd known he was married. It's one of my rules.
DES	*(alarmed)* You haven't... you know... have you?
VAN	No.
DES	Thank God.
VAN	Are you sure he's married?
DES	Of course.
VAN	Promise?
DES	Yes.
VAN	Do you swear?
DES	Yes! Look. I, Desmond Smith, do solemnly swear –

VAN	Desmond?
DES	Yes.
VAN	Is your name Desmond?
DES	Yes.
VAN	Ooh, I love the name Desmond in a man. I've got two rules, Desmond. One, never go with a married man. And two, never miss a Desmond. They just do something for me. I don't know what it is, but I never could resist one – a Desmond.

She starts loosening his tie.

DES	Please…
VAN	Desmond.
DES	Don't…
VAN	You're not married, are you?
DES	No, but Dave is. That's the point. I should know. I was his best man.
VAN	Were you?
DES	Yes, I was. You say he's in his room?
VAN	Yes. *(Smiling)* He's gone to bed.
DES	So where are you intending to sleep?
VAN	Do you really want to know?

DES	I need to know.
VAN	Room 1.
DES	Oh, my God.
VAN	I was just getting undressed... Desmond.
DES	But I thought you just said you didn't go with –
VAN	Watch my lips, Desmond. I was just getting undressed.
DES	Yes, I heard. But I think you'd better come with me.

He takes VAN *by the arm and leads her upstairs.*

VAN	Ooh... Where are we going?
DES	To my room.
VAN	If you say so, Desmond.
DES	*(holding onto his dignity)* I do say so.

DES *holds open the door of Room 2 for* VAN *and she goes in.* DES *shuts the door behind her, goes to Room 1 and knocks.*

DES	Dave? *(No reply. He knocks again)* Dave?

VAN*'s head appears round the door of Room 2.*

VAN	Come on, Desmond.
DES	Just coming.

VAN   Well, don't be long.

                She waves and drops her red blouse
                provocatively outside the door. She goes back
                into Room 2, shutting the door behind her.

DES   Oh, my God.

                Beginning to get desperate, he throws the blouse
                back into Room 2 and locks the door. He returns
                to Room 1 and knocks.

DES   Dave!

VAN   *(off)* Here! What have you locked me in for?

DES   Just a little game.

VAN   *(off)* Ooh!

                DES *knocks again.*

                DAVE *enters furtively DR. He is wearing his*
                boxer shorts, with a T-shirt, and carries his egg-
                coddler. He heads for the stairs. DES *does not*
                see him.

DES   Dave?

                DAVE, *below, hears this.*

DAVE   *(sotto voce)* Damn!

                He changes course and runs off DL.

DES   Dave, come on…

Double or Twin

He exits into Room 1.

*REID enters at the front door in his fishing gear,
with rod and a trout.*

REID   *(singing softly)* "Tonight, tonight... " *(etc.)*

He exits into the cupboard to change.

DES enters from Room 1.

DES   Dave?

*VICAR enters from Room 3 and heads for the
bathroom, carrying sponge bag and towel.*

VICAR   *(musing)*   "Girls, not boys, lead the way –
                 "Double joys: redemption day!"

DES   Have you seen Dave?

VICAR   Who?

DES   Dave. You know, the [tall] chap [with glasses]
(as appropriate).

VICAR   Mr. Reid?

DES   That's the bloke.

VICAR   Didn't he go fishing?

DES   Fishing?

VICAR   Haven't seen him. Sorry.

*He continues along the landing. As he passes
Room 2,* VAN *calls out.*

VAN   *(off)* Desmond... are you coming?

                VICAR *turns.*

VICAR   What did you say?

DES   *(tapping on the wall. Falsetto)* Dreadful...
                bathroom plumbing.

VICAR   Can't help that, I'm afraid. I'm bursting.

                He exits into the bathroom.

                DES *leans over the banister.*

DES   Dave? *(Louder)* Dave?

                REID*'s face appears round the cupboard door.
                He is still changing.*

REID   Hello?

DES   Dave!

REID   Who's that?

DES   *(scampering down the stairs)* Des.

REID   Des?

DES   Yes. Des. There you are.

REID   Can I help you at all, "Des"?

DES   You gave me the slip.

REID   What slip?

DES   At The Trout, you bastard.

             REID *comes out of the cupboard, finishing
             dressing.*

REID   Trout?

DES   Have you got a bird in there?

REID   No, fish.

             DES *rushes into the cupboard.*

REID   Hey! Hey, what are you – ?

             DES *comes out holding* VAN*'s red dress in one
             hand and a fish by its tail in the other.*

DES   *(triumphant)* Aha! A bird *and* a fish!

REID   Excuse me –

DES   She may not be in there now, but I'm keeping
             this as evidence.

             *He stuffs the dress into his jacket pocket and puts
             the fish on the desk.*

REID   Do you mind..?

DES   Her Honour Judge Fish-Pot would be very
             interested in this. No mercy for you then, mate.

She'll have you strung up by your goolies, no sweat.

REID   Fish-pot?

DES   I've got your number, cocker.

REID   That's no secret. It's Willard's Bottom 271.

DES   You made me walk two miles in the mud. And I've told her.

REID   Told who?

DES   The girl.

REID   Who, Val?

DES   I don't care what her name is. I've told her you're married.

REID   Married? Why?

DES   You can't behave like this, Dave. It's not fair. I'm here to keep an eye on you. I promised the Wicked Witch of the North, when she brought me here from the hospital.

REID   *(warily)* Hospital?

DES   Don't play the innocent with me, sunshine.

REID   Excuse me, just what is all this about?

DES   It's about being married.

REID   What?

DES	And you've got to learn to stop this nonsense.
	REID *heads DR.*
DES	Where are you going?
REID	To talk to her.
DES	*(indicating DR)* She's not there. I've locked her in my room.
REID	What do you mean, "locked"? Which room?
DES	Room 2.
REID	What have you locked her in there for?
DES	She's after *my* body now.
	REID *goes up the stairs.* DES *follows.*
REID	You are well out of order, do you know that?
DES	I'm only trying to protect your interests, Dave.
REID	*(turning on him)* And will you stop calling me Dave!
DES	Oh sorry, "David".
REID	"Mr. Reid".
DES	*(mock posh)* "Mr. Reid".
REID	It's you who wants locking up.

Double or Twin

He unlocks Room 2. VAN *peeps out, looking radiant in her nightie.*

REID   *(in love)* Hello.

VAN   *(in spite of herself)* Hi. I thought you were getting undressed.

REID   Did you? Well, I could... I mean... now if you like. Or later...

VAN comes out on to the landing.

VAN   But you're married, aren't you?

REID   No.

VAN   Desmond told me you were.

REID   I'm not married.

DES   *(appalled)* You lying little toad. The things you'll say to get –

REID   *(turning on him)* Shut up, you! *(To* VAN*)* I am not married. I never have been. Not to anybody. Ever. Not even for a short while.

DES   Eight and a half hours is a short while. But it's still a contract.

REID   Don't listen to him. He's mad.

DES   "For better or worse..."

REID   Look, old son –

DES	"For richer or poorer…"
REID	Calm down.
DES	"Till death do us part".
REID	Why don't you go and have a little lie down in your room?
DES	Only if you come with me.
REID	No.
DES	I'm not leaving you alone with a woman.
REID	All right, all right. After you.
	DES *exits into Room 2, expecting* REID *to follow.* REID *locks the door and turns to* VAN. *Muffled abuse from* DES *during the following, which* DES *does not hear.*
REID	I can prove I'm not married. Ask my mother.
VAN	Why don't you ask her?
REID	I can't very well ask my own mother whether I'm married or not, can I? Besides, she can't see me with you in your nightie. Go on.
VAN	I can't. Honestly.
REID	It's important to me.
VAN	Is it?

REID   I don't want to lose you.

                    There is a moment between them, broken by an
                    increase in DES*'s protests.*

VAN   All right.

                    She goes downstairs and knocks on the door DR.

VAN   Mrs. Reid. *(Beat)* Mrs. Reid.

                    She locks more loudly.

FLO   *(off)* Who is it?

VAN   It's me, Mrs. Reid.

FLO   *(off)* What do you want?

VAN   I want to apologise. About tonight.

FLO   *(off)* You can't have your job back, if that's what
                    you want.

VAN   I behaved badly. I never knew your son was
                    married.

                    FLO *throws the door open and enters, forcing*
                    REID *(upstairs) to the floor to avoid being seen*
                    by his mother.

FLO   He's not married. He never has been, he isn't at
                    the moment and he never will be if I have
                    anything to do with it. Least of all to a wanted
                    baggage like you. Go to bed.

Double or Twin

She exits DR.

VAN turns and looks at REID. (DES is silent too). She goes up the stairs and on the landing she and REID kiss long and passionately. They exit into Room 1, putting the "Do Not Disturb" sign on the door, which they lock from inside.

DAVE enters furtively from DL, with egg-coddler. He tiptoes up to Room 1 for his assignation. Just as he reaches the door, DES starts banging again in Room 2. DAVE unlocks Room 2 and DES hurtles out.

DAVE   What are you doing, for God's sake? You'll wake the whole place up.

DES   What did you lock me in for?

DAVE   I didn't lock you in.

DES   Get off, Dave. Or should I say "Mr. Reid"?

DAVE   What are you on about?

DES   Where's the girl?

DAVE   *(evasively, but inadvertently glancing towards Room 1)* Don't ask me. *(Firmly)* I don't know.

DES   She's in there – *(indicating Room 1)* – isn't she? *(Filled with dread)* You haven't... done anything, have you?

DAVE   Chance would be a fine thing.

DES	You expect me to believe that. Standing there in your underpants, the Casanova of Camberwell. Where's your suit?
DAVE	That mad woman made me take it off.
DES	I've heard some excuses in my time –
DAVE	She dragged me away, told me to undress and said, "don't forget to wash your in-betweens".
DES	*(contemptuously)* Ha, ha.
DAVE	I swear it.
DES	You swore a moment ago that you weren't married. "Not to anybody. Ever. Not even for a short while".
DAVE	I think you need locking up.
DES	Ah! You admit it, then.
DAVE	Des, mate, listen
DES	No, you listen. *(Holding up the red dress)* Evidence. Remember? *(Spelling it out, as to an idiot)* Cupboard. Bird. Fish.
DAVE	Fish?
DES	I could use this.
DAVE	I don't think so, mate. It's not your colour.
DES	Dave, I'm serious. Your sweet-tempered mother-in-law might be rather interested in what you've

been up to this evening. And so might Ange. Angelina. Your wife. Remember?

DAVE   Des, you wouldn't…

DES   I don't want you doing anything you might regret.

DAVE   Okay, okay. I'm sorry. She led me on. *(Meaning it)* It won't happen again, Des.

DES   Oh, yes?

DAVE   I swear it.

DES   Barnado's honour?

DAVE   Barnado's honour.

They perform their Barnado Boys ritual.

DES   Look, mate. I know you've had a hard day, what with the wedding, the speeches, and poor Ange's projectile vomiting. I was looking forward to that cake. *(Putting his arm round* DAVE*)* Let's call it a night, eh?

DAVE   You're a good mate, Des.

DES   I couldn't half do with a beer.

DAVE   They've got some downstairs.

DES   You get it. I'm knackered.

DAVE   Right. You take the coddler, okay?

Double or Twin

DES takes the egg-coddler. DAVE goes, stops and turns.

DAVE   Des.

DES   Yeah?

DAVE   Thanks, mate.

He moves to the top of the stairs.

DES takes the "Do Not Disturb" sign from Room 1 and puts it on Room 2 before exiting. (He changes into his pyjamas).

VAL, in her nightie, is thrown out DR. She is followed by FLO, who does not see DAVE.

FLO   I don't know what you're doing back in here, you Decibel. You're supposed to be sleeping elsewhere. Where you belong.

She storms back DR and slams the door.

VAL   But Mrs. Reid –

DAVE starts down the stairs.

DAVE   Hello.

VAL   Mr. Reid. *(Clocking that DAVE is in his underwear)* Oh. Sorry. Have you any idea what's going on?

DAVE   Not really, no.

VAL	Is there anything... I'm sorry to ask you this... anything wrong with her at all?
DAVE	Her? She's mad as a meat-axe.
VAL	Oh, I am sorry. I had no idea. Has she thrown you out as well?
DAVE	I managed to escape. *(Sotto voce)* According to plan. Ready to go, then?
VAL	Go where?
DAVE	Upstairs. You and me. *(Beat)* That's what you want, isn't it?

VAL *backs off.*

VAL	Mr. Reid...
DAVE	Dave. It's Dave. Look, I know I'm married, but only just.
VAL	*(warily)* I don't care whether you're married or not.
DAVE	You don't? Oh, well...

He goes in for a kiss. VAL *slaps his face.*

| VAL | Right, that does it. I've had it up to here. She may not be able to help it. We all know about her sad loss, her arthritis, to say nothing of the cocktail waitress from Weston-super-Mare. She needs treatment. But you have no excuse. I thought I made myself perfectly clear before you went out. I am going to bed. |

Double or Twin

She goes to the desk and looks at the book.

DAVE   Where?

VAL   Room 1, if it's any business of yours.

            She heads for the stairs. DAVE *follows close behind.*

VAL   Why are you following me?

DAVE   Where am I going to sleep?

VAL   Where you always do. Where do you think?

DAVE   It's eighty-four miles to Camberwell.

VAL   *(edgy)* Yes, Mr. Reid.

            VAL, *now seriously worried, backs to the door of Room 1 and tries the handle. (The door is locked from the inside).*

DAVE   What's the matter?

VAL   Please, go away.

DAVE   But I got undressed. Down there. Ready for you.

VAL   It's locked.

DAVE   Is it?

VAL   Look, a joke's a joke. Where's the key?

DAVE   I haven't got it.

> VAL *goes downstairs to the desk, with* DAVE *following.*

DAVE   I left it in the door.

VAL   Well, it's not there now, is it?

DAVE   I assumed you had it.

VAL   Where's the pass key, then?

DAVE   I haven't got a pass key.

VAL   *(increasingly distressed)* You told me that if there was ever any trouble with keys, you'd always got a pass key.

DAVE   I don't know anything about pass keys.

> VAL *breaks down and starts to cry.*

DAVE   Hey, come on. It's all right.

> *He tries to put his arm round her.* VAL *screams.*

VAL   You keep away from me, you sex-maniac!

> DES *rushes out of Room 2 and leans over the banister.*

DAVE   What?

VAL   I never want to see you again.

> DAVE *still tries to comfort her.*

DAVE   Here…

VAL	Leave me alone!
DES	*(a shout)* Dave!
VAL	Oh, it's you. Thank heavens.
	She runs upstairs to DES.
DES	So much for Barnado's honour, you scum-bag. Led you on? You make me sick. *(To* VAL*)* Look, why don't you go back to your room?
VAL	*(tearful)* I can't.
DAVE	She can't get in.
DES	Quiet, you.
VAL	I've got nowhere to go. Room 1's locked and he won't give me the key.
DES	*(to* DAVE*)* Is this true?
DAVE	I haven't got the blasted key.
VAL	See what I mean?
DES	All right, all right. You can have my room for the night.
DAVE	*(coming up the stairs)* Where are we going to sleep?
DES	Will you just shut up for a moment? The young lady's coming with me.
VAL	But where *will* you sleep?

DES   Never mind that. You just get your head down.
           Here's the key. You can lock yourself in. You'll
           be quite safe. *(Gently)* I promise.

VAL   I'm very grateful to you for this. Goodnight.

           There is a moment between them.

DES   Goodnight.

           VAL *exits into Room 2 and locks the door.*

DES   God, you are hard work.

DAVE   Where the hell *are* we going to sleep?

DES   Sofa?

DAVE   Close mates, we may be, Dezza, but dossing
           down with you on my wedding night on a
           draughty flea-ridden settee is a temptation I can
           just about bring myself to resist.

DES   With all due respect, my old cocker, if you count
           the number of available rooms and beds, your
           freedom of choice is seriously limited.

DAVE   *(indicating Room 3)* How about in here?

DES   You can't go in there. That's the Vicar's room.

           DAVE *opens the door and looks in.*

DAVE   It's all right. He's not here. Come on.

DES   What if he comes back?

DAVE	We'll bluff it out.
DES	Dave…
DAVE	He's about a hundred. Deaf as a judge. He'll think he's got the wrong room.
DES	But you can't just –
DAVE	Come on!

He pushes DES *into Room 3, takes the "Do Not Disturb" sign from Room 2 and puts it on the door. He follows* DES *into Room 3.*

MERRYL *enters at the front door.*

REID, *in his boxer shorts and T-shirt, enters from Room 1.*

REID	Won't be a tick. Just going downstairs for some champagne.

MERRYL *clears her throat loudly.*

MERRYL	Excuse me.

REID *comes to the top of the stairs.*

REID	Ah. Sorry. Good evening. Forgive my state of undress. Can I help you at all?
MERRYL	Who's the champagne for?
REID	I'm afraid the hotel is fully booked.
MERRYL	I'm perfectly aware of that.

REID
Then forgive me, but what do you want? It is very late.

MERRYL
I know what time it is, young man. I've come with news of my daughter. I thought you might be interested to know that she's feeling much better.

REID
Your daughter, you say? Good. I'm delighted to hear it. Is there anything else I can do for you?

MERRYL
Have you got a woman in there?

REID
I beg your pardon?

MERRYL
You heard.

REID
I don't see what business that is of yours. What I do off duty's my own affair.

MERRYL
(appalled) Off duty!

FLO *enters DR.*

FLO
David Reid... *(Seeing* MERRYL*)* Oh, it's you again, "Mrs. Smith".

MERRYL
The name is Philpott. Of Philpott's Potted Pastes – pâté providers by Royal Appointment to Her Majesty the Queen. I've come to check up on my son-in-law, and what I find –

FLO
Haven't seen him. *(To* REID*)* I thought I told you to stay in your room, where you belong. Consorting around in your undergarments. This is a respectable house, this is.

REID   Mother –

MERRYL   *(turning on* REID*)* Don't you "Mother" me! It's
              not a blood relationship, young man.

FLO   Come on, you. It's high time you learned to do as
              you were told.

              She crosses and pulls REID *by the ear.*

REID   Ow!

              They exit DR.

              MERRYL, *bewildered, follows.*

MERRYL   I'm sorry... er... could I just have a word?

              She exits DR.

              VICAR *enters, humming, from the bathroom and
              goes to Room 3. He opens the door.*

DAVE   *(falsetto, off)* Leave me alone!

              VICAR *shuts the door smartly, shaking his head.*

VICAR   Ah, sorry, wrong room. I could've sworn...

              He tries the door to Room 2.

VAL   *(off)* Leave me alone!

VICAR   Dear me...

              As VICAR *goes along the landing,* DAVE *enters
              from Room 3, to see* VICAR *exit into Room 1.*

DAVE   It's okay. I told you he was senile. He's gone
              into Room 1.

DES   *(off)* But you said it was locked.

DAVE   Never mind that. At least we've got somewhere
              to kip. *(Putting his head back inside Room 3)* I'm
              off for a slash.

              He shuts the door.

              VAN *screams and backs out of Room 1. As she
              reaches the door of Room 2,* DAVE *turns and
              assumes this is where she's come from.* VAN
              turns as she reaches DAVE *and jumps.*

VAN   Ah!

DAVE   It's all right, it's all right. I'm not going to touch
              you.

VAN   Eh?

DAVE   I promised Des. You look as if you could do with
              a drink.

VAN   I thought that's where you were going.

DAVE   Where?

VAN   To get the champagne.

DAVE   Champagne?

VAN   Yeah.

DAVE   You want champagne?

VAN	Yeah.
DAVE	And you want me to get it for you?
VAN	Yes!
DAVE	Well, if it's champagne you want, my darling, champagne you shall have.
VAN	We are celebrating, after all.
DAVE	Feeling better now, are you?
VAN	I'm feeling wonderful. Now you're back. Chunky!
DAVE	Right... Yes, well... I'll go down and see if there's any champagne, then. You go back to bed, eh?
VAN	I'm not going back in there. I'm going to the bathroom.
DAVE	Okay. Fine. I'll be right back.
	As DAVE *reaches the DL door and* VAN *reaches the bathroom door, she stops him with:*
VAN	David.
DAVE	Yes?
VAN	*(tenderly)* Love you.
	She exits into the bathroom. DAVE *exits DL.*

Double or Twin

MERRYL *enters DR, followed by* FLO, *in violent mid-argument.*

FLO
I don't care whether it's Smith-Philpott or Philpott-Smith. You can get out of my hotel and take your Home Counties bowels with you.

MERRYL
I demand to speak to Mr. Reid.

FLO
You're speaking to nobody, you interfering old trout.

MERRYL
How dare you!

FLO
I've shut him in the bedroom next to mine, where he belongs. And he's there to stay, if it's any business of yours.

MERRYL
I don't think his wife would be very happy about that.

FLO
His wife?

MERRYL
Yes, his wife. At the hospital. They won't let her out. I've just come from there.

FLO
Mental hospital, is it?

MERRYL
You are an offensive woman.

FLO
I should go back to the hospital, if I were you. Where you belong.

MERRYL
Well, really!

FLO
I am locking this door and if you're still here in five minutes, I'm calling the police.

She exits DR and locks the door.

MERRYL   How dare you walk away from me when I'm speaking to you. *(She tries the door)* Will you open this door? … You in there! I'm going to count to three, and you will open this door. One! *(Beat)*

VAL enters from Room 2 on her way to the bathroom.

MERRYL   Two! *(Beat)*

VAL pauses to look at MERRYL over the banister.

VAN enters from the bathroom, unseen by VAL, and has to nip into Room 1 to avoid her.

MERRYL   Three! *(Beat)*

VAL exits into the bathroom.

MERRYL   Four!

VICAR enters from Room 1, having been disturbed by VAN.

VICAR   "Girls, not boys – "

MERRYL   I beg your pardon?

VICAR   "Girls, not boys – "

MERRYL   Who are you?

VICAR	I'm the Vicar. And it's girls, not boys, that interest me.
MERRYL	Then you should be thoroughly ashamed of yourself.
VICAR	Wrong room.
MERRYL	That's my son-in-law's room.
VICAR	My mistake. Bit of a muddle.

VICAR exits into Room 2.

MERRYL	Just a moment. That's Desmond's room. Desmond – that's who I should be talking to. *(Calling as she heads upstairs)* Desmond!

She is halfway up the stairs when DAVE enters DL, with champagne.

DAVE	Darling... *(Seeing MERRYL)* ...Mother-in-law!
MERRYL	How did you get out?
DAVE	Er... just opened the door, really.
MERRYL	*(icily)* So you managed to find some champagne, did you?
DAVE	Er...
MERRYL	There's something very funny going on here, David Reid. *(Pointing in the direction of Room 1/bathroom)* Do you know who's just come out of there?

DAVE	Ah, well… I never touched her. Honestly… She… er…
MERRYL	Who?
DAVE	The woman. I never touched her.
MERRYL	I should think not. She's old enough to be your mother.
DAVE	I'm a married man. You should know. You were there. The wedding. Champagne. This afternoon.
MERRYL	I'm talking about the Vicar.
DAVE	I never touched the Vicar.
MERRYL	No, you stupid boy. He's just come out of your room.
DAVE	The Vicar? Thank God.
MERRYL	What?
DAVE	Thank God for the Vicar. He's been in there all evening. We were terribly worried about him. Agoraphobia. Can't keep him out of women's beds… I mean men's beds… rooms, men's rooms…
MERRYL	And he's gone into Desmond's room.
DAVE	Desmond's room?
MERRYL	Yes, Desmond's room. Are you deaf? Room 2.
DAVE	Room 2?

MERRYL   I think you must be drunk.

DAVE   Drunk?

MERRYL   And will you stop repeating everything I say.

DAVE   Yes.

MERRYL   I shall give a full account of this to Angelina.

DAVE   Angelina? Oh, Angelina. *(Concerned)* How is
                Angelina?

MERRYL   We care about her now, do we? What's brought
                on this sudden bout of compassion?

DAVE   How is she?

MERRYL   Your wife of fully nine and a quarter hours is
                languishing in a hospital bed because you gave
                her a winkle. Whilst you disport yourself in a
                hotel lobby and tasteless underwear, guzzling
                cheap champagne. I don't trust you, David Reid.
                I intend to get to the bottom of this. Where's
                Desmond? *(Calling up to Room 2)* Desmond!
                Desmond!

                DES *enters from Room 3.*

DES   Yes, Mrs. Philpott?

MERRYL   What are you doing in there?

DES   Well, we thought... you see, the Vicar...

MERRYL   Yes, yes, yes. I know all about the Vicar. Is there
                a girl in there?

DES	No. No, Mrs. Philpott.
MERRYL	David, stay there
	She goes smartly upstairs and exits into Room 3.
	VAN *enters from Room 1.*
VAN	Hello, Desmond. *(To* DAVE, *still downstairs)* And hello, big boy. I see you've got the champagne.
DES	*(urgently)* Shh!
DAVE	*(whispering)* Get her into Room 2, quick!
VAN	Why?
DES	Because you're in for a big surprise.
VAN	Ooh, I love surprises.
	DES *shoos her into Room 2.*
DES	She'll search all the rooms.
	VICAR *enters, forced out of Room 2.*
VICAR	Oh. Wrong again, am I?
	He meets MERRYL *at the door of Room 3.*
VICAR	Excuse me, Madam. What are you doing in my room?
MERRYL	You've got a nerve, Vicar, after what I've heard

about your bed-hopping proclivities. I'm looking
for a young woman.

VICAR   Well, we do live in liberal times. Theologically
          speaking, I believe there is no objection to two
          women –

MERRYL   Be quiet, Vicar. Go to bed.

          VICAR *exits into Room 3.*

MERRYL   Right. Room 2.

          She is about to go into Room 2 when DES, *as a
          decoy, gives a girlish giggle from the door of
          Room 1.*

MERRYL   Aha!

          She exits into Room 1. VAN *enters from Room 2.*

VAN   There was a Vicar in there. Are you kinky or
          what?

DAVE   Sorry, darling. The dragon's on the prowl. She's
          checking the rooms.

MERRYL   *(off)* Desmond!

DES   Room 3. Quick!

VAN   *(laughing)* Okay. This is rather fun.

          She exits into Room 3. MERRYL *enters from
          Room 1.*

MERRYL   I definitely heard a noise.

Double or Twin

She exits into Room 2. VAN *enters from Room 3.*

VAN
I'm not staying in there. It's that Vicar again. Ooh, he gives me the willies.

She heads back towards Room 2.

DAVE/DES
(loudly) One! One!

VAN *scampers into Room 1.* MERRYL *enters from Room 2.*

DAVE/DES
(singing) One... derful, wonderful Copenhagen!

The search is over.

MERRYL *leans over the banister to address* DAVE, *downstairs.* DES *is standing beside* MERRYL, *facing the audience.*

MERRYL
Yes, yes, all right. Calm down. It seems that the excitement of the day has led to some high spirits. Now listen to me, both of you. It sticks in my throat to say so, but it appears that I owe you two boys an apology. I am prepared to accept that I may have misunderstood you, David. I may even have been wrong. I shall now return to the hospital to be with Angelina and you may consider the matter closed.

DAVE/DES
Thank you, Mrs. Philpott.

MERRYL
I just need to pop to the bathroom to powder my nose.

She turns to the bathroom and then turns back for a final word.

87

Double or Twin

VAL *comes out of the bathroom and, passing behind* MERRYL *and* DES, *quietly exits into Room 2. Only* DAVE *sees her.*

MERRYL   Angelina and I will be here at 8.30 sharp tomorrow morning.

DES   Yes, Mrs. Philpott.

MERRYL *exits to the bathroom.*

DES *runs downstairs.*

DES   We did it! We pulled it off! Just about gave me heart failure, but we did it!

DAVE   *(almost incoherent)* There are two... Didn't you see them? Two... One's in Room 1 and the other went into Room 2. They're the same. Identical. And they're in there now. Two of them!

DES   What are you on about?

DAVE   There are two girls!

DES   What do you mean, two girls?

MERRYL *enters from the bathroom.*

DAVE   Shh!

MERRYL   *(going downstairs and making for the front door)* Remember. Tomorrow morning, 8.30, on the dot. Make sure the bill's paid and you're packed and ready to go. Good night, Desmond.

DES   Goodnight, Mrs. Philpott.

MERRYL	Goodnight, David.
DAVE	Goodnight, um...

MERRYL *exits by the front door.*

DES	What were you trying to say about the girl?
DAVE	There are two of them. Two girls!
DES	Oh, yeah. And the Vicar's walking across Niagara Falls with a wheel-barrow.
DAVE	It doesn't half explain a lot. *(Belting up the stairs, pushing past* DES *on the landing)* Look, I'll prove it to you.

He goes to Room 2 and knocks.

DES	She's not in there. She's in Number One. *(Not sung)* "Wonderful, wonderful Copenhagen", remember?

DAVE *knocks again.*

VAL	*(off)* Go away!
DES	Hang on. *(Straight to Room 2)* Um. Excuse me, Val. Would you mind coming out here for a moment? It's all right. It's Desmond.

VAL *opens the door cautiously and her head appears. Before she can speak,* VAN *enters from Room 1.*

	Room 1		*Room 2*	
Positions:	VAN	DAVE	VAL	DES

89

VAN   David, where's the champagne? I'm parched.

VAL   *(entering)* Vanessa!

DES   Blimey!

DAVE   See?

VAN   *(crossing* DAVE*)* Val, I'm ever so sorry.
               Everything got a bit out of hand. You know me. I
               mean, he's ever so gorgeous – I couldn't just
               leave, could I? The funny thing is, after what
               we'd been talking about, a Desmond turned up –
               that one – but I still couldn't resist David. That's
               never happened before. No wonder I'm
               confused. And then old Cod Liver Olive turned
               all funny and threw me out. I think I've just lost
               you your job.

VAL   Don't worry, I was leaving anyway. *(To* DAVE*)*
               I hope it doesn't inconvenience you, Mr. Reid, if
               I go in the morning. As soon as I've had time to
               pack.

DAVE   No skin off my nose, darling. We're leaving
               ourselves. First thing.

VAL   What? And never coming back?

DAVE   Not if can help it.

VAN   *(disappointed)* Oh. I rather fancied running a
               hotel.

               Blank looks from DAVE *and* DES.

VAL   Look, I'm off to bed. I've had it.

Double or Twin

VAN	Well, I haven't. *(To* DAVE*)* Come on, chunky. Where's the champagne?
VAL/DES	Oh no…
VAL	There's been quite enough of that for one night.
DES	Too right there has.
VAL	Come on. Girls in Number One –
DES	And boys in Number Two.
	As DES *makes to go into Room 2,* VAL *stops him.*
VAL	Excuse me, I just need to get my things.
	She exits into Room 2.
VAN	*(to* DAVE*)* See you later, big boy. *(Then, as she makes to exit, she whispers in his ear)* Downstairs. Five minutes.
	She exits into Room 1.
DES	What was that about?
DAVE	She wants me downstairs in five minutes. What am I going to do?
	VAL *enters from Room 2 with the spare uniform.*
VAL	Goodnight, Mr. Reid.
DAVE	*(preoccupied)* Er… goodnight.

VAL   And goodnight, Desmond. You've been very
           kind this evening. Thank you.

           She gives DES *a kiss on the cheek and exits into
           Room 1.*

DAVE   So?

DES   *(love-struck)* Mmm..?

DAVE   What am I going to do?

DES   Did you see that?

DAVE   Des..!

DES   What? Oh, don't go. Are you mad? I can see it
           now. Ange turns up in the morning to find you
           and Vanessa the Vamp rolling around half-naked
           on the sofa. Leave it out.

DAVE   Yeah. But what a waste, eh?

DES   If Merryl or Ange so much as set eyes on those
           girls there'll be hell to pay. You know them. I
           lose my job and you lose your wife. Is that what
           you want? So, this is what we'll do. Get up at
           eight, pay the bill and meet them outside. The
           girls will still be asleep upstairs. Merryl and
           Ange need never come in.

DAVE   *(choked)* You're a good mate, Des.

DES   Don't be soft.

           *They perform the Barnado Boys ritual, which
           DES initiates.*

DAVE   Come on.

They exit into Room 2.

REID *enters furtively DR. He makes his way
towards the stairs and stops as* VAN *enters from
Room 1. She leans over the banister.*

VAN   *(whispering)* She's asleep.

REID   *(whispering)* Yes.

VAN   *(running downstairs)* Downstairs, then.

REID   What, here?

VAN   Where else?

REID   On the sofa?

VAN   Mmm.

REID   Whatever you say, my angel.

They embrace.

CURTAIN

Double or Twin

ACT THREE

Sunday. 8 a.m.

*Silence. REID and VAN are asleep, in deep
embrace, under a blanket on the sofa.*

*A very dozy DAVE, still in his boxer shorts and
T-shirt, enters from Room 2. He leaves the door
ajar and exits into the bathroom.*

*VICAR enters from Room 3, in his nightshirt,
still with dog collar, and tries the bathroom
door. It is locked, so he returns to his room.*

*As VICAR's door shuts, REID and VAN wake
up.*

VAN	Hello, darling.
REID	Mmm. Hello.

They kiss.

VAN	Hello!

They kiss again.

An alarm goes off in Room 2.

REID	*(looking at his watch)* My God, it's eight o'clock. Come on, we must get up.
VAN	*(sleepy)* Just another five minutes. It is Sunday.
REID	Yes, and this is a hotel –

VAN	Darling…
REID	And I'm supposed to be on duty.
VAN	Come on…
DES	*(off)* Dave?
REID	Oh, my God.
VAN	What's up?
DES	*(off)* Dave?
REID	It's that bloody man again…

DES *enters from Room 2.*

REID	"Desmond".

DES *sees them over the banister. He is aghast.*

DES	Dave!

He runs downstairs, speechless.

DAVE *enters from the bathroom and returns to Room 2.*

As he passes Room 1, VAL *enters from Room 1 and goes to the bathroom.*

DAVE *shuts the door of Room 2 behind him. He has noticed nothing.*

DES	*(downstairs)* What the hell do you think you're

doing? Are you mad? We agreed. Last night.
You promised to sleep with me.

REID   Oh yes?

DES   Dave, I'm angry.

              VICAR *enters from Room 3 and heads for the
              bathroom.*

VAN   It's all right, Desmond. We're engaged.

DES   Engaged?

VICAR   *(trying the bathroom door)* Engaged? So it is.
              Never mind. Try again in a minute.

DES   I don't believe this.

VICAR   It's true. I've just tried the door.

              He exits into Room 3.

REID   Excuse me. Just what do you think you're doing?

DES   What am I doing? What are *you* doing?

REID   Mr. Smith –

DES   Here we go.

REID   Sod off!

VAN   Look, I'll nip upstairs and get some clothes on,
              okay? *(Getting up, then quietly to* REID*)* Be nice
              to him, darling. He seems a bit upset. See you in
              a min.

She kisses him and crosses to the stairs.

REID   Okay, Val.

DES   Val?

VAN   *(To* DES, *eyes heavenward)* Val! *(Mild reproof to* REID*)* Darling!

She goes upstairs during the following and tries the bathroom door before exiting into Room 1.

REID   I don't know what you –

DES   Look. *(Snatching blanket off* REID*)* You must be stark staring bonkers, mate! *(Quietly and urgently)* We agreed that the safest course, the only course, was to keep them out of the way, not... *(Checking his watch)* Blimey! The old bat will be here in a minute with You-Know-Who. 8.30, remember? I'll go and pack.

REID   *(angrily)* I suggest you do go and pack, and the sooner you're out of here the better.

DES   Listen, I'm trying to help us both. Whatever happens, you mustn't be seen with that girl.

REID   What business is it of yours?

DES   She told me to watch you.

REID   Who?

DES   The boss, who else? She who must be obeyed. The bane of your life and mine, mate, that's who.

REID	Excuse me, that's my mother you're talking about.
DES	Call her your mother if you like.
REID	Eh?
DES	For God's sake go and get some clothes on.
REID	Don't you order me about, you little squirt.
DES	Dave –
REID	Why don't you get out of my life?
DES	What?
REID	Get out of my life!
DES	Dave –
REID	*(livid)* And will you stop calling my Dave!
	VAN *enters from Room 1, dressed in uniform.*
DES	I'm only trying to do what's best for you, mate.
REID	Oh, yeah?
DES	I'm very fond of you, you know.
VAN	That's nice. Getting on better now, are we?
DES	Come on, mate.
	DES *begins the Barnado Boys ritual.* REID *backs off.*

VAN	I'm going to see if I can rustle up some breakfast. Anyone interested?
	She exits DL.
DES	All boys together, eh?
	He tries the Barnado Boys ritual again.
REID	What are you doing?
DES	No hard feelings. Come on.
REID	Will you leave me alone!
DES	What's the matter with you?
	FLO *enters DR with* VAL*'s suitcase ("A") and uniform.*
FLO	This uniform goes to the cleaners tomorrow. To irradiate all trace of her sluttish ways. *(She hangs up the uniform in the cupboard)* Good morning, Mr. Smith. That blanket belongs on the sofa there, if you don't mind, where it belongs. *(To* REID*)* I told that little husky last night, I told her, she had to be out first thing in the morning, bag and baggage. Well, she's the baggage and here is her bags. *(She puts the suitcase by the desk)* Both of you get dressed immediately. I don't want people thinking this is a house for homicidals. Oh, it's a life of grief!
	She exits DR.
DES	Mad!

REID	*("You can talk")* Huh!
DES	*(throwing the blanket at* REID*)* I'm going to pack.
REID	About bloody time. Have you paid your bill?
DES	Oh, it's my bill, is it? No, I haven't had time. Here.
	He takes the wad of £500 from his pyjama pocket and gives it to REID.
REID	What's this?
DES	Five hundred quid. What's it look like?
REID	It's too much.
DES	Are you complaining? It's yours. Take it.
REID	You're giving all this money to me?
DES	Yeah, it's a gift.
REID	A gift?
DES	*(impatient)* A present. Free, gratis and for nothing. Get my meaning?
REID	But...
DES	*(producing the egg-coddler from his other pocket)* And you can take this too.
REID	What?

DES	The egg-coddler.
REID	Egg-coddler?
DES	Oh, for God's sake. Take it.
REID	Carry this thing around with you all the time, do you?
DES	One of us has to have it. That's the rule. Go on, take it.
REID	Me?
DES	Yes.
REID	I don't want it.
DES	Well, I don't want it. It's got your name on it.
	DES *holds it out for him to read.*
REID	Eh? *(Reading)* "David Reid, 22nd of April 19[93]…" It's engraved. With my name. And that's my birthday.
DES	Of course it's your bleeding birthday, you dozy idiot.
REID	How do you know my birthday?
DES	*(exasperated)* Stone me! I've sent you a card every year for as long as I can remember.
REID	You mean it's… from you? Every year? That card I get? D for Desmond?

DES	*(mock stupid)* A for Apple, B for Banana, C for Cat, D for Desmond! Oh, this is silly. I know everything about you, mate. I should do. I've been following you around for years.
REID	You keep away from me.
DES	I've had enough of this. *(Starting to go upstairs)* They'll be here in a minute from the hospital. I'm going to have a quick leak, then I'm getting packed.
REID	Fine.

REID *is nonplussed, holding the money.*

VAL *enters from the bathroom and blows* DES *a kiss before exiting into Room 1.*

DES	*(to himself)* What a sweetheart.
REID	Watch it!

DES *exits into the bathroom.*

VICAR *enters, still in his nightshirt, from Room 3 and makes for the bathroom.*

VICAR	David! Good morning, good morning!
REID	Oh. Good morning, Vicar. Sorry about my… er…
VICAR	Not at all, dear boy, not at all. God created the body as well as the soul. "*Mens sana in corpore sano*", what?
REID	What?

Double or Twin

VICAR	Big day for you today. Mum's the word, but I've got a feeling in my water. Talking of which...
	VAN enters DL.
VAN	*(to* REID*)* Fancy some breakfast?
VICAR	How kind. I'll be down in a moment.
	He tries the bathroom door. It is locked.
VAN	*(to* REID*)* All right, darling?
VICAR	*(returning to his room)* I'll manage, dear. I'll manage.
VAN	*(to* REID*)* What's the matter?
VICAR	Still engaged.
	He exits into Room 3.
REID	*(meaning* DES*)* He's potty.
VAN	No, just a bit deaf, that's all. Are you all right?
REID	Yeah, yeah. Listen, I want you to have this.
VAN	What is it?
REID	Five hundred pounds.
VAN	Are you giving me money?
REID	Yes.
VAN	You bastard!

REID	Eh?
VAN	What kind of girl do you think I am?
REID	No, no, no. You don't understand. It's for you. To buy a ring. That's what the money's for. For you. For us. Take it. I know we only met yesterday, but I've never been more sure about anything in my life. I meant what I said last night. I… I want you to marry me. *(Beat)* Will you?
VAN	*(taking the money)* If you think you're up to it!
REID	You should be the best judge of that!
VAN	Oh, David!
	They kiss.
	DES *enters from the bathroom. He stays on the landing.*
DES	Get packing, you moron!
REID	*(patiently)* I'm not packing. You're packing, remember?
DES	I'm not doing your packing.
REID	*(exploding)* I'm not packing!
VAN	Boys, boys! And you were getting on so well just now. *(Heading DL)* Breakfast is ready when you want it.

Double or Twin

REID *collects suitcase "A" and heads for DR door.*

VAN *(to* DES*)* He's buying me a ring.

She exits DL.

DES *(beside himself)* Ring? Ring? Where are you going with that suitcase?

REID I'm putting it back where it belongs. It's the young lady's, if it's any concern of yours.

He exits DR.

DES Ring? *(Coming downstairs)* Dave...

VICAR *enters from Room 3.*

VICAR Still engaged, I expect.

DES *(impatiently)* Yes, Vicar.

VICAR *(a joke)* Well, normally I'm all in favour of long engagements, but –

DES *(furious)* Don't speak to me about engagements, you stupid old goat! He's giving her a ring now!

VICAR Oh yes? What's her number?

DES He knows my job's on the line, too.

VICAR Nine-two-what?

DES Totally out of order.

VICAR	Well, if it's out of order, we're all jiggered.
	He exits into Room 3.
DES	God Almighty.
	FLO *enters DR with suitcase "A" and takes it to the desk.*
FLO	*(muttering)* Bag... baggage... over my dead body. *(Seeing* DES*)* Aren't you dressed yet, Mr. Smith? Persons in their pyjamas belong in the privy of their own bedrooms, where they belong... Oh, it's a life of grief!
	She exits DR.
DES	*(checking at his watch again)* Don't let it happen. Please don't let it happen. I like my job. I like Angelina. I like Dave. Please God let him come to his senses.
	VAL *enters from Room 1, still in her nightie.*
VAL	I can't find my uniform.
DES	Where did you last have it?
VAL	It was in my room.
DES	I think Vanessa's wearing it. She's getting breakfast.
VAL	*(coming downstairs)* Never mind. I've got some clothes downstairs. I'm not staying in this madhouse a moment longer. Desmond, I still haven't thanked you properly for last night. I

	don't know what I'd have done if you hadn't been there, really I don't.
DES	It was nothing, honestly.
VAL	No, I mean it. Thank you, Desmond.
	She kisses him on the cheek.
VAL	Don't go without saying goodbye, will you?
DES	I certainly won't.
	REID *enters DR, now dressed in shirt and trousers (Note: not the same clothes as last night)*
REID	I thought you'd got dressed.
VAL	Not me.
	REID *comes straight up to her, embraces her and kisses her on the upstage cheek.*
VAL	*(embarrassed, but smiling)* No. You've got the wrong one, Mr. Reid.
REID	If you insist.
	He kisses VAL*'s other cheek.*
VAL	No. I'm Val.
REID	I know you are, darling.
	He goes for a kiss on the lips. VAL *slaps his face.*

VAL	Stop it! Will you just stop it!
	She storms off DR.
DES	What the hell do you think you're playing at? Going after Val now, are you? I think you need help, mate. I really do.
REID	I'll go after who I like, you little twerp.
DES	*(grabbing* REID*'s shirt-front)* Now you listen to me, sunshine. I've had it up to here with you. I am going to say this once, and once only. Touch that girl one more time and you'll need your jaw fixing.
REID	You take your hands off me.
DES	Have you got that?
REID	I'm warning you.
DES	And I'm warning you.
REID	Right. That does it.
	He slugs DES.
REID	And if you're still here when I get back, I'll really hit you.
	*He picks up suitcase "A" and exits DR. (*DES *is too dazed to notice his exit)*
DES	Blimey!

Double or Twin

VICAR *enters from Room 3, dressed. He comes downstairs.*

VICAR	"Girls, not boys, lead the way". *(Seeing* DES*)* Ah, it's you. Today's the day!
DES	I don't know how to get through to that man.
VICAR	Ring Telecom. They'll fix it. I must go and feed the inner man.

He exits DL.

DES *wanders round in a daze as* DAVE *enters from Room 2 in shirt and trousers (the same as* REID*'s). He carries two suitcases ("B" and "C"), which he puts by the desk.*

DAVE	Come on, mate. Hurry up. It's nearly half-past. I thought you'd be ready and dressed.

DES *starts growling quietly.*

DAVE	You all right? *(No answer)* How are you getting on with Val then, you old dog?
DES	*(quietly)* What?
DAVE	You're well in there, Des old cocker. Always the quiet ones.
DES	Come here.
DAVE	What do you want?
DES	*(dangerously)* Just come here.

109

DAVE

Des..?

DES hits DAVE hard. DAVE falls behind the sofa.

DES

Nice one, Dezza.

VAL enters DR, still in her nightie.

VAL

I thought you said Mr. Reid was your friend. He's behaving very strangely.

DES

You can say that again. Val, look, I'm sorry –

VAL

I think he's stolen my clothes now. My room's been cleared.

DES

He's done some funny things in his time, but dressing up in women's clothes isn't one of them.

VAL

What am I supposed to do?

DES

(looking at his watch) My God, it's nearly time.

VAL

Time for what?

DES

You can't stand there with nothing on.

VAL

You're one to talk.

DES takes the uniform from the cupboard and goes upstairs with it.

DES

Come on, you can wear this. Don't worry about a thing. I'll sort Dave out. He's not himself this morning, that's all.

Double or Twin

VAL	*(following him upstairs)* What's the great hurry?
DES	Well, you can't change down here, can you?
VAL	No, but what's the rush?
DES	His mother-in-law's coming at 8.30. That's now. She's my boss. She made me swear to keep him in order. If she sees you running around with next to nothing on she's bound to jump to the wrong conclusion. I'll lose my job. What's more, she's bringing his wife with her.
VAL	So he has got a wife?
DES	Yes.
VAL	Are they divorced?
DES	Not yet they're not.
VAL	Separated?
DES	No.
VAL	Then why don't they live together?
DES	They're going to, after the honeymoon.
VAL	Haven't they been on honeymoon yet?
DES	No, well, she got ill, didn't she. Been in hospital.
VAL	He never said. Doesn't he care about her?
DES	I thought he did. Now I'm beginning to wonder.

VAL	Well, we can't have you losing your job. What do you want me to do?
DES	Nothing. Just keep out of the way till they've gone. And please – get dressed!
VAL	All right. But it's for you, not for him.

She takes the uniform to Room 1.

DES *stops her with:*

DES	Val.
VAL	Yes?
DES	You're a diamond.

VAL smiles and exits into Room 1.

DES *runs downstairs and kneels on the sofa, back to the audience, and leans over, talking to the prostrate (and invisible) DAVE.*

DES	Dave.

REID *enters DR, crossing DL.*

DES	Dave!

REID *stops CL.*

DES	I'm sorry, Dave. Come on. Quick. The women will be here in a minute.

Double or Twin

REID *is appalled. Turning, he sees suitcases "B" and "C" by the desk. He picks them up angrily.*

DAVE *groans.*

REID *exits hurriedly DR.*

DAVE *groans again. He comes up from behind the sofa.*

DAVE   Des, old son. What was that for?

DES   We're quits now.

DAVE   Eh?

DES   I'm worried about you, mate. Just promise me one thing: you'll leave Val alone.

DAVE   Val?

DES   Yes. Val. Do you promise?

DAVE   If you insist.

DES   I do insist.

DAVE   Blimey, you have got it bad. Yeah, I promise.

DES   Right, better get a move on. Merryl and Ange will be here any minute. Val's promised to keep out of the way. We could just be okay.

DAVE   Have you paid the bill?

DES   Of course not.

DAVE   What?

DES   I gave the money to you.

DAVE   No, you didn't.

DES   I did.

DAVE   No jokes now, Des. Please.

DES   Jokes, "Mr. Reid"? I'm serious.

DAVE   Are you feeling all right?

DES   Am I feeling all right? I slept in my own bed last night. *(VAN's voice)* "It's all right, Desmond, we're engaged!" *(Own voice)* Engaged, my arse! *(VAN's voice)* "He's buying me a ring!" *(Own voice)* I've heard that one before. Do you think I'm stupid? *(Mock stupid again)* "A for Apple, B for Banana, C for Cat". *(Own voice)* How do I know your birthday? Have I paid my bill? Well, you can get out of my life, sunshine. And you can take your blasted egg-coddler with you!

    He thrusts the egg-coddler at DAVE.

DAVE   What's going on?

    MERRYL *enters at the front door.*

MERRYL   Yes, what is going on?

    DAVE *and* DES *freeze.*

MERRYL   Desmond, what are you doing standing about in your pyjamas? Why aren't you dressed? It's half-

past eight. Angelina's waiting in the car. We're
ready to go. David's dressed. I'm disappointed in
you, Desmond. Disappointed. David, why isn't
Desmond dressed?

DAVE   I don't think Desmond's very well.

MERRYL   *(to* DES*)* Winkles?

DES   Pardon?

MERRYL   Winkles.

DES   Ah. *(Suddenly holding his stomach)* Yes.

MERRYL   "Never trust a prawn, an oyster or a winkle!"
              And what I don't know about crustaceans is not
              worth knowing. Have you paid the bill?

DES   )   Yes
) *(together)*
DAVE   )   No.

MERRYL   What?

DES   )   No.
) *(together)*
DAVE   )   Yes.

MERRYL   Is the bill paid, Desmond?

DES   No, Mrs. Philpott.

MERRYL   Give me the five hundred pounds. I'll deal with
              it.

DES   No, Mrs. Philpott.

MERRYL	What?
DES	I mean, Phil, Mrs. Yes-pot... Flip, Mrs. Whatsit... I mean, not yet, Mrs. Sexpot.

VAN *enters DL and stays by the door.*

VAN	Darling, do you want breakfast or not?
DES	Oh, my God.
MERRYL	David, who is this girl?
DAVE	She's... er... this hotel. The, um, receptionist. Isn't she, Des?
VAN	Oh, you silly! I'm not really the receptionist.
MERRYL	Desmond, who's the girl?
DES	She's...
DAVE	His...
DES	My..?
DAVE	Fiancée.
DES	My fiancée?
DAVE	Your fiancée.
DES	My fiancée.

VAN *slaps* DAVE*'s face.*

VAN	Ooh!

Double or Twin

FLO *enters DR, carrying suitcases "A", "B" and "C".*

VAN	I'm not engaged to him. I'm engaged –
FLO	Nor will you never be, while I've got cod left in my liver, you scheming little conductress! *(To* DAVE*)* David, open the front door.

DAVE *opens the door.*

FLO	Engaged, my eye! Nothing but a cover-up for fortification and lust. And I should know.

She throws all three cases outside.

FLO	Well, that's the little bag's baggage. *(To* DES*)* Are you advertising pyjamas, Mr. Smith? *(Looking at* MERRYL*)* I see Loopy Lou's back. David, ring the hospital and get them to cart her away. Oh, it's a life of grief!

She exits DR.

MERRYL	Well, really! Desmond, go and get dressed.
DES	*(not moving)* Yes, Mrs. Philpott.
MERRYL	Now!
DES	Yes, Mrs. Philpott.

He heads upstairs. As he goes:

DES	*(to* DAVE, *meaning* VAN*)* Get her out of here.

A car horn is heard outside.

DAVE	That's Ange.
MERRYL	David, come here.

A second blast of the horn.

DES *exits into Room 2.*

MERRYL	This girl. Is she or is she not Desmond's fiancée?

DAVE)   Yes
) *(together)*
VAN   )   No.

MERRYL	If she is, why wasn't I told? And if she isn't, then who is she?

A longer blast on the horn.

MERRYL	Oh, blast! Angelina needs me. I shall want a word with you in a minute, young lady. David, stay here.

MERRYL *exits by the front door.*

VAN	Me, engaged to your little friend? What did you say that for?
DAVE	I'm sorry, I had to say something.
VAN	I'm not speaking to you any more.

She exits DL.

DAVE	*(frantic)* Dezza!

He runs to the window to check on MERRYL.

Double or Twin

VICAR enters DL.

VICAR   Could I pay my bill, do you think?

DAVE   Not now, Vicar.

He exits DL.

REID enters DR and crosses to the desk.

REID   Don't forget to pay your bill, Vicar.

VICAR   Dear boy... Dear Lord... Didn't you just..? The other...

REID   Yes, Vicar.

VICAR   But... how did you..?

REID   No hurry, Vicar. Whenever you're ready.

VICAR   *(turning in excitement and running upstairs)* I thought I saw... It must be a sign. Today's the day! Let us pray for the manifestation of this miracle. Let us pray! I'm coming, Lord! I'm coming!

He exits into Room 3.

REID   Mad as a hatter.

MERRYL enters at the front door.

MERRYL   David.

REID   Oh, you've turned up again, have you?

MERRYL	What's all this about Desmond's fiancée?
REID	No idea. How's the potted paste business?
	DES *enters from Room 2, still in his pyjamas.*
MERRYL	Be quiet. When did they get engaged?
DES	Excuse me…
MERRYL	And what's her background?
REID	How's your lovely daughter this morning?
MERRYL	This is no time for silly games.
DES	Mrs. Philpott…
MERRYL	It is half-past eight.
REID	My goodness, so it is.
MERRYL	I came straight from the hospital.
DES	I can't find my suitcase.
REID	The hospital?
MERRYL	Of course. Where else?
DES	I can't get dressed if I haven't got my suitcase.
REID	I see. *(Quietly)* You've come to take him away, have you? *(He taps the side of his nose)*
MERRYL	What are you doing?

REID	*(with a wink)* Discretion in front of the patient.
MERRYL	Are you feeling all right?
REID	I'm feeling fine. It's him you should be worried about.
MERRYL	It was only a winkle. Now tell me. Plain question, plain answer. Who is that girl?
REID	Why don't you mind your own business?
DES	Dave!
MERRYL	It is my business, you odious man. I am Angelina's mother.
REID	You could be Boadicea's great-aunt for all I care. You walk in here like Lady Muck –
MERRYL	How dare you!
REID	Throwing your weight around as if you owned the place –
DES	*(running downstairs, forgetting about suitcases)* Dave!
REID	You keep out of this. *(To* MERRYL*)* Just who the hell do you think you are?
MERRYL	You will live to regret that remark.
REID	Are you threatening me?
MERRYL	Yes, I am.

DES	She'll go mad.
REID	*(checked)* Mad? Oh, my God. Mad, yes... *(To MERRYL)* Did you say you'd come from the hospital too?
MERRYL	Yes, I spent the night there. You know I did. I could hardly leave, could I?
REID	Couldn't you? No, no. I suppose you couldn't.
MERRYL	I've had enough of this nonsense. Desmond, you stay here if you like, but David is coming with me.
REID	*(humouring her)* Oh yes? Where am I going, then?
MERRYL	Tunisia. Three o'clock flight. We haven't got time to stand around here all day. Are you ready to leave?
REID	Well, as you said, it is half-past eight.
MERRYL	At last! Now, is there somewhere down here I can go to powder my nose?
REID	Ah. Yes, there is as a matter of fact. Through that door there.

He steers MERRYL to the cupboard.

| MERRYL | Thank you. |

She goes in. REID locks the door.

| DES | You've locked her in! |

REID	Have I?
DES	You can't do that.
REID	*(humouring him)* No, no. Of course I can't.
DES	You're going about this the wrong way, mate. I know we didn't want Angelina to see the girls, but –
REID	Angelina?
DES	Your wife, remember?
REID	From the hospital too?
DES	Yes, from the hospital. For heaven's sake, have you taken leave of your senses?
REID	Coming to Tunisia too, is she?
DES	That was the general idea.
REID	Fine. Okay. If you say so.
DES	I do say so.
REID	We'll all go to Tunisia together, shall we?
	MERRYL *hammers on the cupboard door.*
MERRYL	*(off)* David. Why have you locked me in this cupboard?
	DES *makes for the cupboard.*
REID	Don't let her out!

DES	Are you mad?
	VAL *enters from Room 1, dressed in her uniform.*
VAL	Is the coast clear?
DES	No. Wait.
REID	I'm warning you. Go anywhere near that cupboard...
DES	I think you've cracked.
	DES *goes to open the cupboard.*
REID	I warned you.
VAL	*(coming downstairs)* What's going on?
	REID *hits* DES *over the head with a warming pan (or some convenient ornament).* DES *is dazed, but standing.*
REID	It's all right. I've got him.
VAL	You beast!
REID	Eh?
	VAL *grabs a vase from an alcove in the staircase wall and breaks it over* REID*'s head.*
VAL	Take that!
	REID *falls.*

MERRYL   *(off)* What is going on out there?

DES   *(dazed)* She mustn't see you. She mustn't see
                you. She's in the car.

VAL   No, she's not. She's in the cupboard.

DES   He locked her in the cupboard, not the car.

VAL   *(leading* DES *upstairs)* It's all right, Desmond.

DES   No, she's out there! She's out there!

VAL   Come along. You've got a nasty bump. I'll bathe
                it for you.

DES   My suitcase is full of winkles.

MERRYL   *(off)* Would somebody kindly let me out of this
                cupboard!

DES   That woman gave me five hundred pounds.

                VAN *enters DL.*

VAN   What's happening?

DES   She's my Philpott's potted boss.

VAL   I slugged your fancy man, that's what. He's gone
                too far this time. Come along, Desmond.

                VAN *rushes to* REID *and cradles his head.*

DES   Pâté providers to Her Majesty the Queen.

                VAL *and* DES *exit into the bathroom.*

VAN   Darling, are you all right? It's me, Vanessa!

                She starts kissing REID *on the mouth.*

                ANGELINA *enters at the front door. She is 21,
                strong and very pretty – a good match for*
                DAVE.

ANGELINA   Hello.

VAN   *(without looking up)* Hello.

ANGELINA   What are you doing?

VAN   Giving him the kiss of life. He's just been hit
                over the head.

ANGELINA   Stand aside. I'm a qualified nurse. *(Approaching)*
                Darling…

VAN   "Darling"?

ANGELINA   Can you hear me?

                REID *groans.*

ANGELINA   He's just a bit concussed. He'll be all right.

                REID *starts to get to his feet.*

ANGELINA   That's it. Steady. On your feet. You've taken a
                bit of a knock. You're probably still feeling
                woozy. Can you hear what I'm saying, darling?

REID   *(to* VAN*)* Darling.

ANGELINA   Poor love. He doesn't even recognise me.

VAN	Who are you?
ANGELINA	I'm his wife.
VAN	His wife?
REID	Where's my mother?
	He staggers DR.
REID	Where's my mother?
	He exits DR.
ANGELINA	Poor sweetheart. He gets so upset about his mother. He lost her at an early age.
	She follows REID *off DR.*
VAN	Bastard!
	There is a banging from the cupboard.
MERRYL	*(off)* Will somebody open this door!
VAN	Hello?
MERRYL	*(off)* You out there. I shall count to three, and if you don't open this door, I'll... One! ... Two! ...
	VAN *goes to the cupboard and unlocks it.* MERRYL *comes out.*
MERRYL	Three! Ah, it's you. What have you been doing with my son-in-law?
VAN	So it's true, he is married. The swine.

MERRYL	Have there or have there not been any shenanigans with my daughter's husband?
VAN	The pig!
MERRYL	I asked you a plain question and I expect a plain answer.

DAVE *enters DL.*

DAVE	Oh, my God.
VAN	But how did you..? I thought you went... Didn't you just..?
MERRYL	David, did you or did you not spend the night with this girl?
DAVE	No.
VAN	Oh!
MERRYL	Do you swear?
DAVE	Yes.
VAN	Ooh, you low-down, lily-livered, lousy little liar!

She slaps DAVE's face hard and runs up to Room 1 in tears.

MERRYL	So, what have you got to say for yourself, young man?
DAVE	*(dazed)* I'm going to get packed before the dragon arrives with the champagne. She mustn't find us here with the girls. She mustn't. *(Going*

upstairs) Never trust a prawn, an oyster or a mother-in-law.

VICAR *enters from Room 3 and meets* DAVE *on the stairs.*

VICAR   Don't forget about the bill.

DAVE   It's all right. I'll pay it.

             DAVE *exits into Room 2.*

VICAR   That's very good of you. On the house, eh? I suppose there isn't any coffee on the go? *(To* MERRYL*)* What a nice young man.

             He exits DL.

             MERRYL *makes to follow* DAVE *upstairs.*

MERRYL   David!

             ANGELINA *enters DR.*

ANGELINA   David's not very well, mother. He doesn't even recognise me. I'm a bit worried.

MERRYL   You have every right to be worried, my dear. I'm going to get to the bottom of this. Stay there.

             She heads upstairs.

ANGELINA   Mother –

MERRYL   Don't move. I'm going to have a word with the girl.

ANGELINA   Mother –

MERRYL   Angelina, enough!

            FLO *enters DR.*

FLO   It's that woman again.

            MERRYL *exits into Room 1.*

FLO   She's barmy, do you know that? Stark, staring
            bonkers. She's from the hospital. She told me
            last night. Nutty as a suitcase. Who are you,
            anyway?

ANGELINA   I'm Mrs. Reid.

FLO   No, you're not.

ANGELINA   Pardon?

FLO   I'm Mrs. Reid.

            REID *enters DR.*

REID   Mother!

ANGELINA   *(putting her arms round* REID) Darling..?

FLO   Don't you "darling" him. There've been far too
            many she-nanny-goats in this house already.

            ANGELINA *kisses* REID.

REID   Oh, I don't know!

            .

Double or Twin

ANGELINA   Darling, I hope you're packed. I'm dying to get off to Tunisia.

REID   Tunisia? Oh, my God. You must be Angelina. From the hospital. You were in the car. Outside. He said so. The chap in the pyjamas.

ANGELINA   *(gently)* That's right, darling.

REID   You keep away from me!

ANGELINA   *(worried)* Darling..?

FLO   Be quiet, you! David, Mad Margaret's back. She's gone into Room 1. Lock her in.

REID   *(aside to* FLO*)* I think we'd better lock them all in and inform the authorities. There's the mad woman upstairs, this one here who wants to take me to Tunisia, and the little maniac in the pyjamas who'll take me anywhere for five hundred pounds. Leave this to me.

MERRYL *enters from Room 1.*

MERRYL   David!

REID   My God, it's her.

MERRYL   It appears you haven't been telling me the whole truth. Where's Desmond? I demand to speak to Desmond.

REID   Er... I think he popped into Room 3.

MERRYL   What for?

REID	To have a word with the Vicar. On a spiritual matter.
MERRYL	You'd better be telling me the truth.
	She knocks on the door of Room 3 and goes straight in.
	REID *bounds up the stairs and locks her in.*
REID	Got her!
ANGELINA	What did you do that for?
REID	*(running downstairs)* She was getting in the way a bit, "darling". I thought you and I should have a moment or two together. Before we go off to Tunisia.
ANGELINA	*(laughing)* Darling, you are awful. She'll be livid.
REID	Yeah, but it's only for a couple of minutes, eh?
ANGELINA	I can see you're back to normal, anyway. I was getting worried. Kiss, please.
REID	*(indicating* FLO*)* Not here. *(Taking* ANGELINA *upstairs)* Upstairs. Quickly. Come on, Room 2's free. *(Reaching the door of Room 2)* Close your eyes.
ANGELINA	What are you doing?
REID	A little surprise, that's all. No peeking.
ANGELINA	You know I like surprises!

Double or Twin

REID *steers her into Room 2 and locks the door.*

REID *(running downstairs)* That's two of them. Now, where's the little lunatic in the pyjamas?

As he reaches the bottom of the stairs, VAL *enters from the bathroom, followed by* DES.

REID *(hiding from* DES*)* Ah...

VAL You just go and have a little lie down in your room.

DES *tries the door of Room 2, unlocks it and goes in.*

VAL *continues downstairs.*

FLO You still here? I thought you'd gone.

VAL I'm leaving as soon as someone tells me what's happened to my luggage.

REID *(aside to* VAL*)* It's okay. I've put your cases back in your room.

VAL *(frostily)* Thank you, Mr. Reid.

She exits DR.

REID *races upstairs with the intention of locking Room 2.*

REID Now we've got him!

The door of Room 2 opens and DES *backs out.*

DES   *(to* DAVE, *in Room 2)* Sorry, Dave old mate, sorry. Didn't know you were in there.

He shuts the door and turns to face REID. *Double-take. He backs away R.*

DES   My God! How did you..? But you're in... with Angelina... Aren't you?

He faints dead away in front of Room 1. REID *re-locks Room 2.*

REID   He's passed out.

VICAR *enters DL.*

VICAR   Now, Flo...

FLO   *(to* REID*)* Lock him up! Quick!

VICAR   Why, what have I done?

FLO   Be quiet, Vicar.

REID   I think he's dead.

VICAR   Dead? Who's dead?

DES *groans.*

FLO   Of course he's not dead. Lock him up.

REID *drags the half-comatose* DES *into Room 1.*

VICAR   Can I help?

FLO   We've caught the maniacs, Vicar.

VICAR	Oh, I am sorry.
FLO	*(to* REID*)* I'll ring the hospital.
VICAR	I think you'd better.
	VAN *storms out of Room 1 and marches downstairs.*
VAN	Can't you leave me alone, you bastard?
	REID *enters from Room 1, locking the door behind him. He follows* VAN.
VAN	I'm fed up with the lot of you, I'm off. Where's my sister?
REID	Sister?
FLO	Sister?
VICAR	Sister!
FLO	*(pointing DR)* I think she went…
VAN	Thank you.
	She exits DR.
REID	Wait a minute…
	He follows VAN *off, amazed.*
FLO	Sister?
VICAR	"Girls, not boys…" They are the girls, Flo. Don't you see? The vision is coming true. The dream I had the night your boy was lost.

FLO	I shall never forgive myself, Vicar. That fateful day. My little David. Spirited away. Egg-coddler and all.
VICAR	Share my faith, Florence. "That which is lost shall be found!" Your David is alive.
FLO	I don't want to talk about it, Vicar.
VICAR	Half the vision is fulfilled. The girls are here. So where are the boys?
	There is loud banging from MERRYL *in Room 3.*
MERRYL	*(off, but loud)* Will someone let me out of this room!
VICAR	A voice from above!
	He hurries upstairs. (He remains on the landing for the rest of the play).
FLO	Don't let her out, Vicar. She's mad.
VICAR	"Knock and the door shall be opened unto you!"
	More knocking. VICAR *unlocks the door of Room 3.* MERRYL *enters.*
MERRYL	Where is Desmond?
	Banging from Room 1.
MERRYL	I want to speak to Desmond.
FLO	Oh, put a sock in it will you!

MERRYL	I shall be suing you for wrongful imprisonment, you miserable, working-class hag.
	VICAR *unlocks Room 2.*
FLO	You'll pursue nobody once you're back in your padded cell, where you belong.
	More banging from Room 1.
FLO	Don't let him out, Vicar. He's madder than she is.
VICAR	So much the better. Let the mad go free!
	He unlocks Room 1. DES *enters.*
MERRYL	Desmond!
DES	*(gibbering)* D-d-d-
VICAR	"They spoke in tongues and God saw that it was good!"
DES	D-d-d-Dave… Dave… He's got a…
VICAR	Yes, yes, yes!
	VAN *and* VAL *enter DR, followed by* REID.
DES	In there… It's amazing… He's got a…
MERRYL	Desmond. Pull yourself together.
VAL	Desmond..?
DES	Twi-twi-twi-

VAL	Are you all right?
DES	Twi-twi-
REID	Mother, look! This explains everything.
DES	Twin!
REID	It's wonderful!
VICAR	"See the works of the Lord and all his wonders!"
DES	*(madly jumping up and down)* There are two!
REID	Oh, God...
DES	There are two!
VICAR	That's right. And here they are.
DES	*(running downstairs)* No. Men. Men. Men!
REID	Who let him out?
VICAR	It was God's will. We must all be witnesses to the miracle! "Girls, not boys, lead the way. Double joys – "
MERRYL	Silence!

She comes downstairs.

MERRYL	You've gone too far this time, David Reid. I'm cancelling Tunisia and I'm having the marriage annulled. Where is Angelina? *(Calling)* Angelina!

Double or Twin

ANGELINA *enters from Room 2, unseen by all except the* VICAR. *She is open-mouthed with wonder as she sees* REID.

REID   Marriage? What marriage? I'm not married.

During the following choral attack, VAN, VAL, DES *and* MERRYL *form a semi-circle around* REID, *upstage of him.*

MERRYL   How dare you!

DES   *(to* REID*)* Dave?

MERRYL   You'd deny your own mother if you knew who she was.

DES   Is it you?

MERRYL   There were two hundred witnesses. Desmond was your best man.

VAL   I wish you'd make up your mind whether you're married or not.

VAN   You bastard! Did last night mean nothing to you?

REID *puts his hands over his ears. The next three speeches are spoken together.* MERRYL *starts,* VAL *joins, then* VAN. *During this,* REID *collapses into a foetal position, facing the audience.*

MERRYL   Thank God we found out before you wrecked my daughter's life. The wedding you so conveniently deny cost me ten thousand pounds. I always knew you weren't good enough for

Angelina. Her poor father must be turning in his grave. But at least she knows who her parents are!

VAL   I know Vanessa can be a bit wild at times, but she deserves better treatment than this. You never could take no for an answer, could you, Mr. Reid?

VAN   I don't know what to believe. What about this engagement ring we're supposed to be getting?

REID   *(screaming)* Stop!

All three speeches end simultaneously.

Silence.

DAVE *enters from Room 2.*

DAVE   What's going on?

All but REID *face upstage, stunned.* REID, *facing the audience hears his 'own' voice.*

DAVE *comes slowly down the stairs, followed by* ANGELINA. *Seeing* DES *with* MERRYL *and* FLO, *he fears exposure, but is determined to bluff it out.*

DAVE   Well, come on. What's happening? Why are you all staring at me? Des? Mother-in-law? Are we off?

REID *stands and turns towards* DAVE.

REID   Brother?

Double or Twin

DAVE	Brother?
REID	Brother!
	A moment of amazement.
FLO	My son!
DAVE	Mother?
FLO	David!
DAVE/REID	*(together)* Yes?
	FLO *crosses to* DAVE.
FLO	David. My son.
REID	No, mother. I'm David.
DAVE	Mother?
FLO	Yes, David.
DAVE	Mother!
	FLO *and* DAVE *embrace.*
VICAR	What did I tell you, Flo? Your David is alive!
REID	Hang on a minute. His name can't be David.
DAVE	Yes, it is. *(Producing his egg-coddler)* And I've got my egg-coddler to prove it.
FLO	You've kept your little egg-coddler all these years!

Double or Twin

REID	My name's David.
FLO	*(to* REID*)* It isn't, my son. You're not David.
REID	What's my name, then?
FLO	It's on your egg-coddler.
REID	Eh?
FLO	Twenty-eight years ago we lost your brother and his coddler on your christening day. I swore to the Vicar that I wouldn't let your egg-coddler out of my sight until toddlers and coddlers were reunited. From that day on I called you David, after your lost twin. It kept his memory alive in my heart, and only your egg-coddler bears your true name.
REID	What is my true name?
FLO	*(taking the coddler from her pocket and handing it to him)* Your name, my son, is –
REID	*(reading)* Desmond.
VAN	Desmond?
DAVE/DES/VAL	Desmond!
VAN	I knew it! *(Coming to him)* I've always wanted to marry a man called Desmond.
MERRYL	Would somebody kindly explain to me which of these two young men, if either, was recently married to my daughter.

VAN   Yeah, that's a point. *(To* DES*)* You told me last
        night he was married.

DES   Yes, well…

DAVE   *(warning)* Des.

DES   No, I didn't. Not married. I mean, I thought you
        meant the other one. Not… not that I knew there
        was another one, of course. When you asked. I
        couldn't have done, could I? I mean, there was
        only one girl then. There were two afterwards, I
        know. I said *he* was married. I mean, if you
        thought he wasn't married, you might have
        wanted to… marry him… sort of…

VAN   Well. *(Holding up the money)* I've got five
        hundred pounds here that a certain somebody
        gave me this morning.

MERRYL What?

VAN   I wonder who it was.

DAVE   That's my five hundred pounds.

VAN   Oh, my God.

REID   But I gave it to you.

ANGELINA *(to* DAVE*)* Then why did you say it was yours?

DAVE   It was. But Desmond had it.

VAN   Which Desmond? My Desmond or her
        Desmond?

143

DAVE	Her Desmond. My Desmond. The Desmond in the pyjamas.
DES	*(To* DAVE*)* But I gave it to you.
REID	No, you didn't. You gave it to me. This morning. To pay the bill.
DES	Five hundred quid, for one night in a hotel? We didn't even get breakfast.
VICAR	I got breakfast!
MERRYL	*(taking the money from* VAN*)* Give it to me. I entrusted this money to Desmond.
DES	And I gave it to Dave.
DAVE	Only I didn't want it.
DES	So he gave it back to me.
REID	Then this morning he gave it to me.
DAVE	Because he thought you were me.
REID	And I gave it to Vanessa.
VAN	To buy an engagement ring.

ALL *ex.* MERRYL Oh, I see.

Beat.

FLO	So who paid the bill?
VICAR	It's all right. He let us off.

FLO	Oh, it's a life of grief!
MERRYL	David, did you or did you not give that girl my five hundred pounds?
ANGELINA	Mother.
MERRYL	Yes?
ANGELINA	Enough.
	DAVE *moves to* REID.
DAVE	Brother!
REID	Desmond, David.
DAVE	Desmond!
REID	David!
DAVE	Dave, Desmond.
REID	Dave!
DAVE	Desmond!
	They embrace.
FLO	Bless you, Vicar. I always said my little David would be found.
VICAR	Ah, Flo!
ANGELINA	*(to* DAVE*)* Darling!
	They kiss.

VAN	*(to* REID*)* Darling!

They kiss.

VAL	*(to* DES*)* Darling!

They kiss.

VICAR	My friends, let us rejoice.
MERRYL	Stop! I can be silent no longer. Mrs. Reid –
FLO	Yes?
MERRYL	It was I who stole your baby all those years ago. My name was Cheryl then – Cheryl Smith – head chorister at the church where the christening was to have taken place. I was just seventeen. I wanted a baby so badly. I saw you go into the vestry, to adjust your hat, and on a sudden impulse I took your little twin. It was a terrible thing to do, I know. I travelled abroad to escape detection. Then some months later I gave birth to my own little boy. I decided to call him Desmond, because Desmond was the name of the little companion from whom baby David had been parted. I so wanted them to be happy, you see. I struggled to bring them up on my own, but the strain was too great. So one day, the saddest day of my life, I left them at an orphanage where I knew they would be safe. I made a new life for myself. Cheryl Smith became Merryl Smythe. I blocked out my old life completely and for ever, or so I thought. Until a year ago, when my Angelina brought David and his friend Desmond home, with the tale of their abandoned childhood. There they were, the baby I'd stolen

and the son I had borne. I knew that instant it
was them, the coincidence was too great. But I
couldn't allow myself to know, could I? I
couldn't acknowledge it, even to myself.

DES   So…

MERRYL   Yes, Desmond. I am your mother.

DES   Mother!

MERRYL   My son!

They embrace.

DES   Who was my father?

VICAR   Desmond!

DES   Vicar?

MERRYL   Cecil? Is it really you?

VICAR   Cheryl, my beautiful chorister. May God forgive
               me.

MERRYL   He will! He has!

VICAR   Cheryl!

MERRYL   My dear Florence. Can you ever forgive me?

FLO   Forgive? Rather rejoice with me – for I have
               found my sheep that was lost.

VICAR   Let us all rejoice!

FLO   Oh, it's a life of...

           ALL *look at* FLO.

FLO   Joy!

           CURTAIN

           OPTIONAL NOTE: At the curtain call, a twin
           likeness of the VICAR *may appear on the*
           landing and join him for his final bow (and
           maybe even triplets for the two sets of twins –
           from understudies?)

Printed in Great Britain
by Amazon

57103657R00090